Luftwaffe: Birth, life and death of an air force

Luftwaffe: Birth, life and death of an air force

Alfred Price

Pan/Ballantine

Editor-in-Chief: Barrie Pitt
Art Director: Peter Dunbar

Military Consultant: Sir Basil Liddell Hart
Picture Editor: Bobby Hunt

Executive Editor: David Mason
Designer: Sarah Kingham
Cover: Denis Piper
Research Assistant: Yvonne Marsh
Cartographer: Richard Natkiel
Special Drawings: John Batchelor

Contents

Goliath brought down

Introduction by Generalleutnant Adolf Galland

It is not easy to give a concise account of the activities of the German Luftwaffe during the Second World War. And since this account is concentrated in the 160 pages of this book, it must be limited to a description of the essential strategic and tactical concepts and a general outline of the course of events.

In the present volume, Flight-Lieutenant Alfred Price has undertaken this memorable and historically important task with knowledge and intelligence.

The objective nature of his description, which sometimes seems almost too cool, is enriched by short interspersed accounts of personal experiences which give the whole a fascinating texture. This will without doubt convey a vivid image even to those readers who may not be familiar with the historical sequence of events.

After the spectacular rise of the Luftwaffe, from its first splendid successes which made Hitler's Blitz-

krieg possible until the end of the campaign in France, there followed a long agony, interrupted only by occasional successes. Price leaves open the question of whether this change was due to a lack of general direction and to intrigues among the leaders; but he treats the problem attentively. He feels that the decline in the Luftwaffe's fortunes shows that the air battle over Britain constituted a turning point: destroying the myth of the invulnerability of the Luftwaffe, and taking a high toll among its peacetime-trained and battle-proved crews. His assessment of the Battle's results is correct in both aspects, although in the first instance he obviously missed the key to the fundamental causes. The German Luftwaffe was a tactical force, not a strategic one, in Douhet's terminology. It was when it was used as the latter that it was bound to fail. The second result is undeniable. The squadron commodores and leaders,

the group commanders of the years to come, all died in the air battle over Britain.

When Price gives an objective and detached account he succeeds in fascinating. Where he makes value judgments he may occasionally leave himself open to disagreement. This is no criticism, however, rather an advantage, for fruitful discussions may develop.

Overall, this book amounts to a considerable accomplishment. Even if the operations the author describes seem relatively antiquated in the light of technical progress and contemporary nuclear strategic theories, they are still a living bit of history – which at the least will be thought-provoking. Beyond this, the book furnishes a number of suggestions which may stimulate more detailed research and critical appraisal. Perhaps one or another among the young German historians will take up the thread from here. It would be desirable.

The rebuilding of an air force

Formation of Heinkel 51 fighters,
pictured shortly after the unveiling of
the Luftwaffe, in 1935

Under the Treaty of Versailles, which brought the First World War to its final humiliating end for the Germans, military aviation was prohibited in that country. The construction of civil aircraft was also banned until 1922, after which it was allowed but with certain limitations regarding weight, ceiling, speed and horsepower. But although they were forced to work at a sharp disadvantage, the Germans somehow managed to retain their proficiency in building and flying aircraft. And perhaps because the field of military aviation had been forbidden to them, the German public maintained an unusually high degree of air-mindedness.

In 1924 General Hans von Seeckt, the chief of the Army General Staff, succeeded in placing his own candidate, Hauptmann Ernest Brandenburg, at the head of the Air Office of the Ministry of Transport. Now co-operation between the highly centralised German civil aviation organisation and the armed forces was assured, and from then on the development of civil aviation in Germany was largely controlled and directed with military interests in mind.

As time passed restrictions imposed by the Treaty of Versailles on the training of service officers as pilots were gradually relaxed. By 1926 the Germans were permitted to train a maximum of ten pilots per year from the army – ostensibly for the purpose of gathering meteorological data, and also to provide aerial support should the German civil police need it.

Also by 1926 the restrictions on aircraft construction had been lifted. A small but efficient aircraft industry was already in being, and by this time there existed almost all the firms which were later to mass-produce aircraft for the Luftwaffe: Dornier at Friedrichshafen, Focke Wulf at Bremen, Heinkel at Warnemunde, Junkers at Dessau. And at Augsburg a young designer named Willi Messerschmitt was hard at work producing designs for sporting aircraft for the Bavarian Aircraft Company.

By the amalgamation of several financially unsound air transport companies the new state airline *Lufthansa* was formed, an airline which enjoyed government sponsorship. Already the various smaller airlines had been flying regular schedules to the Eastern European countries. Now, under a series of agreements with Germany's previous enemies, *Lufthansa* was allowed to establish routes in Western Europe. The company developed and improved its night and all-weather flying techniques, and technically it became one of the most advanced in the world. Shortly after its creation, a small nucleus of military crews was formed within the state airline. These military crews trained at the four *Lufthansa* flying schools, but the need to pay lip-service to the dictates of the Treaty of Versailles prevented tactical training taking place in Germany.

For their more warlike activities, the German pilots went to Russia. Under a secret treaty concluded with the Soviet government in 1926, German fighter, bomber and reconnaissance crews were allowed to use the military airfield at Lipetz, some 200 miles south of Moscow. Flying green and gold painted Dutch-built Fokker D-XIII fighters innocent of national insignia, the German pilots worked out tactics for the air battles of the future. It was also at Lipelsk that the prototypes of the new German combat aircraft underwent their weapons trials, notably the Heinkel 45 and 46 reconnaissance machines, the Arado 68 fighter and the Dornier 11 bomber. In each case the guns and bomb racks had to be removed from the aircraft before they left for their transit flights to Russia, but these were shipped to Lipelsk separately and refitted there.

But, as in all air forces during the late 1920s, the Germans were short of money, and only a few crews were trained in Russia. Meanwhile, back in Germany, army officers kept a close watch on developments in the more advanced and less fettered air forces.

This, then, was the position when Adolf Hitler gained power in Germany in 1933. The bare foundations for a military air arm existed, but there was a long way to go before it could become a force to be reckoned with. But Hitler knew well that a powerful air force would be an essential pre-

requisite if he was to achieve his
stated aim of expanding the German
Lebensraum (living space). So, almost
immediately after the new government took office, the pace of the
development of military aviation
quickened. Hitler's deputy, Hermann
Göring, became amongst other things
the new *Reichskommissar* for Air. But
Göring was also an important political
figure in the National Socialist Party,
and was able to devote little time to
aviation matters. So the greater part
of the work of forging the new weapon
fell to his deputy, Erhard Milch.

Milch was faced with an enormous
task. But to achieve it he received the
full support of the Nazi government,
and all the money and resources he
could reasonably use. Under the
strictest secrecy he set up new training schools, ordered the building of
new airfields and factories, and placed
large orders for aircraft with the
various German firms. The very size
of his requirements caused a ripple to
run through the entire aircraft industry. For example, at the beginning of
1933 the capacity of the Junkers
company, one of the larger German

**Hitler, Göring and Milch, during the
acceptance ceremony of
Jagdgeschwader 134 into the
Luftwaffe on 20th April 1935**

aircraft companies, was sufficient to
produce only eighteen Ju 52 transports per year; Milch placed an
immediate order for 200, to be completed within two years. Other companies received similar orders, and
generous state aid to build and equip
new factories.

The first of the new fighters Milch
ordered into large-scale production
was the Heinkel 51, a biplane with a
top speed of 210 mph which carried an
armament of two 7.9mm machine guns.
To equip his bomber force he ordered
two types, the Dornier 23 and the
Junkers 52 – both of them converted
transports. But so far as Milch was
concerned these machines were merely
interim types; they would serve to
open up the production lines, and
provide his crews with experience on
reasonably modern aircraft. The 1930s
brought with them a revolution in
aircraft design, as the fabric-covered
strut-braced biplane with its fixed

11

Above left: Ju 52 airliner of Lufthansa, the German state airline. *Below left:* He 51 fighters, wearing civil markings, prior to the unveiling of the Luftwaffe. *Above:* Focke Wulf 44 trainer

undercarriage gave way to the much faster monoplane with a fully cantilevered wing, retractable undercarriage, variable pitch propeller and all-metal stressed skin construction. Milch's aim was to have a force ready to receive the new generation of combat aircraft, when these became available. To meet this end the initial emphasis in the new air force was on training, and nearly half the aircraft ordered were training machines: Focke Wulf 44's, Arado 66's, etc.

By March 1935 the Germans felt sufficiently strong to reveal their previously secret air force to the world. The Luftwaffe now comprised a total of 1,888 aircraft of all types, and mustered 20,000 officers and men. One by one the unusually professionally-run 'flying clubs' and 'police formations' were handed over to the new air force, during glittering ceremonial parades, some of which Hitler himself attended. Abroad, these developments were viewed with grave

misgivings, and in turn each of the European nations began to rearm in response to the new threat. The arms race had begun.

At this stage, let us take a closer look at the men who filled the leading positions in the new Luftwaffe.

At the head of the force was Hermann Göring, then an extremely forceful and energetic political leader approaching the height of his power and prestige. As Hitler's closest friend and confidant since the earliest days of the National Socialist Party, his position was unassailable. A First World War fighter ace with twenty victories to his credit, he felt himself to be well qualified to speak on aviation matters; but in fact his years away from flying after 1918 had left him with a poor understanding of the great changes which had taken place in aviation since the war. Above all else an egotist, Göring tended to take everything to do with the new service personally; he was

General Walter Wever was the first
Chief of Staff of the Luftwaffe

Following Wever's death, General
Albert Kesselring filled the post

reluctant to admit that any task was
beyond the Luftwaffe, and even more
reluctant to seek advice from his
subordinate officers. But against all
that, Göring was able to use his
political influence to secure for the
Luftwaffe a useful priority over the
army and the navy in the allocation
of resources. As a result of this and
his uncompromising manner, he remained permanently at loggerheads
with the commanders-in-chief of the
other two services.

Directly under Göring was State
Secretary Erhard Milch, an untiring
and efficient worker as well as a sound
business man. Before he joined the
Luftwaffe Milch had been the director
of the state airline *Lufthansa*, and
this had given him an intimate
knowledge of the operation of aircraft
which served him well when he came
to build up the air force.

Subordinated to Milch was the Chief
of the Air Command Office, General
Walter Wever, an ex-infantryman
who had transferred to the new
Luftwaffe. Wever was an unswerving
disciple of National Socialism; he is
reported to have said on one occasion
that the Luftwaffe officer corps would
either be National Socialist, or it
would not be at all! But in spite of,
or perhaps because of, his extreme
political views, Wever applied himself
to his task with great zeal; at the age

of forty-six he learnt to pilot an
aircraft, and became as enthusiastic
in his new found skill as any of his
subordinates. Wever was an extremely
capable staff officer, and his work did
much to sooth the growing pains
unavoidable in the new force. Moreover, by dint of great tactfulness, and
a willingness to remain in the background if necessary, Wever was able
to stay on good terms with both
Göring and Milch.

Under this trio the Luftwaffe developed swiftly.

By 1936 the second generation of
German combat aircraft, the ones to
replace the initial, interim types,
had begun their flight testing. The
standard single-engined interceptor
fighter was the Messerschmitt Bf 109,
and for the long-range 'destroyer' role
there was the heavier twin-engined
Messerschmitt Bf 110. The standard
bombers were the Dornier 17 and the
Heinkel 111, and for short-range dive
bombing there was the lighter and
simpler Junkers 87. All these types
were sound modern designs, and when
they appeared they stood at the very
forefront of aviation technology.

In May 1936 General Wever was
killed in an air crash. His loss was a
severe blow to the Luftwaffe, and
Göring was quite sincere when he
afterwards stated:

'He [Wever] was not a man to

Generalmajor Hans Jeschonnek was Chief of Staff when the war began

remain within the four walls of his study, unknown to his troops. On the contrary, he was an inspiring example to us all – straightforward, modest, and yet a great man and a fine officer. His contribution cannot be adequately described with mere words. The fact that the Luftwaffe exists to day is due to his untiring work – to his outstanding contribution.'

In Wever's place Göring appointed the Chief of the Luftwaffe Administration Office, General Albert Kesselring, and the post was renamed 'Chief of the General Staff'. Like his predecessor, Kesselring proved to be a strong and popular commander. The expansion of the Luftwaffe proceeded apace.

In August 1936 the new German air force went into action for the first time, in support of General Franco's Nationalist forces rebelling against the Spanish Republican Communist government. Initially the German air support comprised a mere twenty Junkers 52 transports, together with an escorting force of six He 51 fighters. But these few aircraft were able to have an effect on events far beyond their meagre numbers. General Franco desperately needed to move troops loyal to him from Morocco to mainland Spain, and move them quickly. By flying as many as four round trips in a day, and carrying some twenty-five fully equipped men on each trip, the Ju 52 force rapidly moved in 10,000 fighting troops. It was the first time that an airlift operation on such a large scale had ever been mounted, and it was sufficient to consolidate Franco's shaky position.

But it soon became clear that the insurgents would need much more in the way of help. In the months that followed the Luftwaffe contingent swelled, and by November the force, now named the *Legion Kondor* (the Condor Legion), comprised some 200 aircraft; one half of these were Junkers 52 bombers and Heinkel 51 fighters, while the rest was made up of reconnaissance, ground attack and transport machines. The force was able to achieve little during the early months, because the He 51 proved to be an inferior fighting aircraft when it was pitted against the more modern Russian-built Polikarpov I-16 monoplane fighters used by the Republicans. But during the summer of 1937 the Germans moved in their latest types, the Bf 109 fighter and He 111 and Do 17 bombers, and with these the Condor Legion soon gained air superiority over Spain.

Over Spain the German fighter units were allowed complete freedom to develop their own tactics. They had begun by flying in the close wing-to-wing formations used by the Italians, but soon found these tactics – which had survived with little change since the First World War – to be impractical with the much faster monoplane fighters. The Messerschmitt pilots found that they had to watch each other so carefully, to maintain position and avoid collisions, that they had little time left to keep watch for the enemy. Eventually the loose 'finger four' formation, worked out by Oberleutnant Werner Mölders, was found to give the best compromise between concentration of fire power on the one hand, and freedom of action on the other.

For the most part the fighter missions over Spain were mounted to escort bomber attacks on positions well behind the Republican lines. If they had fuel left after completing this primary task, the Messerschmitt pilots would sometimes turn back and carry out strafing attacks on enemy

15

Above and Below: It was during the war in Spain that the new Luftwaffe first saw action; Legion Kondor He 111s bomb Republican targets

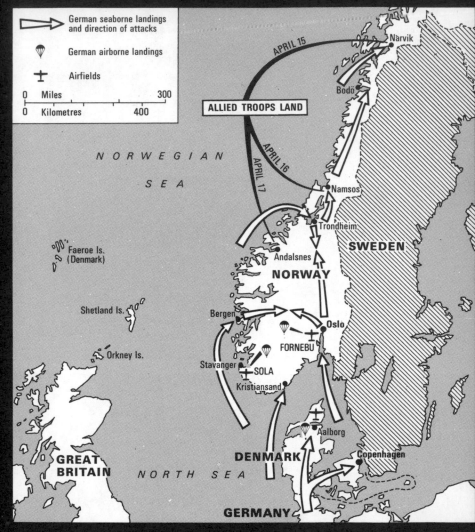

German and Allied attacks in Scandinavia

Above: The Bf 109 fighter was blooded in action in Spain. *Below:* Göring reviews men of the Legion Kondor after their return from Spain; behind him stands General Wolfram von Richtofen

Above: Dornier 17 bombers in formation. *Below:* Heinkel 70 high speed reconnaissance aircraft

Above: Junkers 86 diesel-engine powered heavy bombers. Below: Henschel Hs 123 dive bombers of Sturzkampffgeschwader 165

The Heinkel 51
He 51: *Engine:* one B.M.W. VI, developing 750 hp for take off. *Armament:* two 7.9mm machine guns. *Maximum speed:* 206 mph. *Ceiling:* 23,500 feet. *Range:* 370 miles. *Span:* 33 feet 9 inches. *Length:* 25 feet 8 inches

airfields before they returned to their bases. On a few occasions the German pilots mounted fighter sweeps over Republican territory. When Republican fighters rose to the bait, large air battles often resulted, and then the Messerschmitt pilots were able to use their superior mounts to good advantage.

One development in Spain which did have an important effect on future German policy was the use of the He 51, obsolescent as a fighter, as a ground attack aircraft. The load of four 22-pound bombs, plus a droppable fuel tank with a special igniter, was dropped 'by eye' on the targets which were usually front line objectives such as roads, bridges, trenches and troops. The aircraft would go in at low level,

at about 500 feet, in close formations of up to nine machines, and all the pilots would release their loads when they saw the formation leader nod his head vigorously. These tactics usually succeeded because at this time air attack had a fearful effect upon ground troops, who usually kept their heads down when aircraft were in sight. The Chief of Staff of the Condor Legion, Oberst Wolfram Freiherr von Richthofen (a cousin of the famous First World War fighter ace) pioneered these new methods; in some of the small-scale actions then being fought they proved decisive. Later, these same tactics would prove equally effective in much larger actions.

The war in Spain ended in March

1939, and the men of the Condor Legion returned to Germany. But in the meantime a major crisis was brewing up in Central Europe.

In March 1938 German troops marched into Austria, and the following September Hitler was allowed, as a 'last territorial demand', to annex a large slice of western Czechoslovakia. In March 1939 German forces occupied the remainder of the country. By then it was becoming clear that Hitler's next target would be Poland – whose frontiers were guaranteed by Britain.

Meanwhile, there had been considerable behind–the–scenes diplomatic activity, as both Germany on the one hand, and Britain, France and Poland on the other, sought out allies, or at least 'non-enemies', for the conflict which seemed to be drawing closer with each day that passed. Most countries preferred to keep well out of the argument, but the Germans did succeed in getting a military alliance with Italy, and later in securing a non-agression pact with Russia.

In May 1939 Hitler decided that the time had come to strike. His forces, newly trained and equipped, had a margin of strength over their opponents which would never be greater. On the 23rd of the month he calmly informed the commanders-in-chief of his three fighting services that he intended '. . . to attack Poland at the first suitable opportunity'. War was now inevitable.

On the eve of war

Do 17s fly low over the Nuremburg Stadium, during a tattoo held before the war

By summer 1939, then, Hitler had made up his mind to go to war with Poland to settle his differences. And, since the governments of both France and Britain had stated that in the event of a war they '. . . would lend the Polish government all support in their power', there was every likelihood that the conflict would not remain confined to Eastern Europe.

On 1st September 1939 the Luftwaffe possessed 3,650 combat aircraft:

LEVEL BOMBERS
(mainly Do 17 and He 111)   1,170
DIVE BOMBERS
(Ju 87)   335
SINGLE-ENGINED FIGHTERS
(Bf 109)   1,125
TWIN-ENGINED FIGHTERS
(Bf 110)   195
RECONNAISSANCE AIRCRAFT
(mainly Do 17 and Henschel 126)   620
COASTAL TYPES
(He 59, He 60 and He 115)   205

As war became inevitable, the Germans stepped up the production of combat aircraft. *Below:* **Do 17 fuselages near completion.** *Right:* **Bf 109s**

In addition there was an aircraft reserve of between ten and twenty-five per cent of the first-line strength, depending upon type. Backing this combat force and its reserve was a training organisation with more than 2,500 aircraft, plus a further 500 operational types used for operational training.

The aircraft which made up the backbone of the bomber and fighter arms, respectively the He 111 and the Bf 109, were decidedly better than any equivalent in large scale service in any other air force. In terms of training and morale, too, the German crewmen were the equal of any, and superior to most, of their opponents.

Thus far the picture is impressive. But there were certain deep-seated weaknesses – weaknesses which were to have a profound effect upon the German ability to wage a long war in the air.

First, let us take a look at the changes that had taken place at the top of the Luftwaffe during the last two years of peace.

As we have seen, Kesselring had taken over the post of Chief of the

Above: Henschel 126 battlefield reconnaissance aircraft. *Above right:* Heinkel 115 reconnaissance and torpedo floatplane. *Below right:* Junkers 88 high speed long range dive bomber

General Staff in 1936, following Wever's death. But gradually friction had developed between Kesselring and his immediate superior, Milch, and after a year in the post the former asked Göring to relieve him. Kesselring moved out to command the Third Air Administrative Area *(Luftkreis III),* and in his place came the previous head of the Luftwaffe Personnel Office, Generalmajor Hans-Jürgen Stumpff. But Stumpff in his turn found the new task very heavy going, for the steady expansion of the force made necessary a series of far-reaching organisational changes which left him little time to get to know his subordinates. Moreover, he had little more success in his relations with Milch than did Kesselring, and with similar results.

In the meantime, Milch's own position, and the confidence and favour he enjoyed with Hitler, had aroused the emnity of Göring, who saw in his deputy a possible rival for his leadership of the Luftwaffe. As Milch has told this author: 'Some of the people in the Nazi party began to say that I was the real head of the air force, not Göring. They said this not because they liked me particularly – but because they hated him!' Göring reacted to this imagined threat by bringing others into his circle of confidants, and also by divesting Milch of some of his powers and the influence they gave him. In short order Milch lost his direct control over the Air Staff and also the technical and personnel departments.

To ensure a tight hold over the Technical Office, Göring placed an old friend of his, Ernst Udet, at its head. Udet was one of the most colourful characters in the new Luftwaffe; still a brilliant aerobatic pilot, he had ended the First World War with sixty-two kills to his credit as the top-scoring German pilot to survive the conflict. Since the early part of 1939, Udet had held the post of Chief of Air Force Procurement and Supply *(Generalflugzeugmeister),* with the rank

Immediately before the war the Bf 109-equipped units made up the backbone of tho Luftwaffe fighter arm

of Generaloberst. But for all his endearing qualities – he was a very clever cartoonist, and often amused his guests with this and displays of trick shooting – Udet was a sad misfit in his highly important post. He tended to concern himself too much with technical 'gimmickry', and with the aerobatic qualities of the new types under evaluation for the Luftwaffe, all at the expense of his main responsibilities for comprehensive testing and production. Udet could have made good use of Milch's advice on technical and administrative matters, but Göring saw to it that the paths of communication between the two men were kept long and tenuous.

Stumpff had left his post as Chief of the General Staff in February 1939 and in his place came the fourth officer to hold this position since 1935: Oberst, shortly afterwards Generalmajor, Hans Jeschonnek. Jeschonnek was a protege of General Wever, who had picked him out as being a man of outstanding intelligence and ability. Moreover, like Wever himself, Jeschonnek was an ardent National Socialist. At the age of thirty-nine the new Chief of the General Staff was a very young man to be filling such an important post, and his youth placed many difficulties in his path. He was a lonely person, and he failed to achieve any sort of rapport with either Milch or Udet. Moreover, because of his youth, Jeschonnek found himself unable to prevail upon the more senior *Luftflotte* commanders, who did not hesitate to use their personal friendships with Göring to overrule him. Göring knew full well that he was intellectually inferior to the younger man who now headed his staff, but this served only to increase his reluctance to consult Jeschonnek before he announced his decisions. The net result of all this was that Jeschonnek found himself in the invidious position of being responsible for much of what happened in the Luftwaffe, while at the same time he had little real power to influence events.

Thus it came about that the four

A Heinkel 111 crew prepares for a flight from Jever, in August 1939

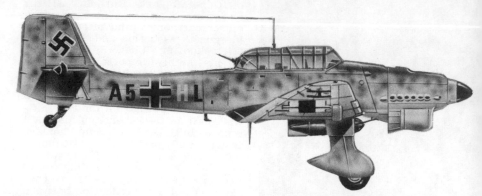

The Junkers Ju 87

During World War II the tactical dive-bomber was most successfully exemplified in the Junkers Ju 87. Although the type was often called the Stuka, this word is in fact a contraction of the German word *Sturzkampfflugzeug,* meaning 'dive bomber'; thus the term *Stuka* refers to all dive bombers and not to any particular one. Remarkably successful against unprepared enemy troops early in the war, when the Germans usually had air superiority, the Ju 87-equipped units suffered heavy losses when they were engaged by determined fighter pilots flying modern aircraft. Specification for the Ju 87B-2: *Engine:* Junkers Jumo 211, developing 1,200 horse power for take off. *Armament:* either one 1,100 pound bomb or one 550 and four 110 pound bombs; three 7.9mm machine guns. *Maximum speed:* 238 mph at 13,400 feet. *Ceiling:* 26,200 feet. *Range:* 370 miles with a 1,100 pounds bomb. *Weights:* empty, 5,980 pounds; loaded, 9,560 pounds. *Span:* 45 feet 3½ inches. *Length:* 36 feet 5 inches.

The Heinkel He III

Numerically the most important bomber in the Luftwaffe during the first half of the war, the Heinkel He 111 saw service on all fronts. By the end of 1941 it was becoming out-dated, but because of development difficulties with the He 177 which should have replaced it, the older type continued in service until the end of the war. Also used as a transport and a glider tug. Specification of the He 111 H-6. *Engines:* Two Junkers Jumo 211s, each of which developed 1,340 hp for take off. *Armament:* up to 4,400 pounds of bombs was the normal load, but in the overload condition a single 5,500 pound bomb could be carried; one 20mm cannon and five 7.9mm machine guns. *Maximum speed:* 258 mph at 16,400 feet. *Range:* 760 miles with maximum normal bomb load. *Ceiling:* 25,500 feet. *Weight:* empty, 17,050 pounds; loaded, 27,400 pounds. *Span:* 74 feet 1½ inches. *Length:* 54 feet 5½ inches

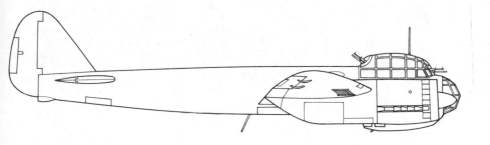

Junkers Ju 88

The Junkers Ju 88 was the most versatile aircraft to see service with the Luftwaffe, and operated as a bomber, day and night fighter, ground attack aircraft, torpedo bomber and reconnaissance aircraft and, at the very end of the war, as a flying bomb. Some 15,000 examples were built. Specification of the Ju 88A-1: *Engines:* Two Junkers Jumo 211, each developing 1,200 hp for take off. *Armament:* up to 3,300 pounds of bombs; four 7.9 mm machine guns. *Maximum speed:* 280 mph at 18,000 feet. *Range:* 620 miles with normal bomb load. *Ceiling:* 26,250 feet. *Weights:* empty, 16,975 pounds; loaded, 22,840 pounds. *Span:* 60 feet 3½ inches. *Length:* 47 feet 1½ inches.

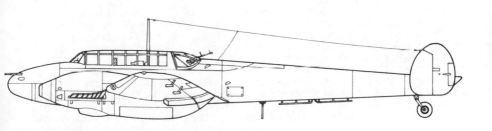

The Messerschmitt Bf 110

Originally conceived as a long-range bomber destroyer, the Messerschmitt Bf 110 proved successful in that role and also as a night fighter. However, when it was used as an escort fighter during the Battle of Britain it was a failure, due to its poor manoeuvrability compared with the opposing British single-engined fighters. The 'Bf' in the designation stood for *Bayerische Flugzeugwerke* – Bavarian Aircraft Company – where designer Willi Messerschmitt's aircraft were built. Specification for the Bf 110C: *Engines:* Two Daimler Benz DB 601As, each developing 1,100 hp for take off. *Armament:* two 20mm cannon and four 7.9mm guns in the nose; one rearwards-firing 7.9mm machine gun. *Maximum speed:* 349 mph at 23,000 feet. *Ceiling:* 32,000 feet. *Range:* 565 miles at 300 mph at 23,000 feet. *Weight loaded:* 15,300 pounds. *Span:* 53 feet 4¾ inches *Length:* 39 feet 8½ inches men at the top of the Luftwaffe on the eve of the war – Göring, Milch, Udet and Jeschonnek – were in each case either ill-fitted or else unable to carry out their proper tasks. Moreover, each of the men was at loggerheads for much of the time with the other three. For his part Göring made no attempt to change this state of affairs but actually encouraged it, so that he might more easily divide and rule over his subordinates.

In spite of all this, the foundations laid by Milch and Wever were firm enough to withstand the disruptive pressures generated inside the force prior to the war. Later, when these pressures were combined with those exerted from outside by the enemy, this paucity of leadership was to have serious consequences. For the Luftwaffe was to be administered, rather than led, into battle by its high command.

Given these divisions at the top, major errors were not long in coming. One of the most important of these was to be the decision from Jeschonnek that all bombers after the Do 17 and the He 111 must be able to dive-bomb. The problems caused by this decision will soon become clear to the reader. But first, let us consider the reasons behind it.

There are two ways of increasing the effectiveness of a bombing attack using high-explosive bombs: first, one can use bigger aircraft or a greater number of smaller ones, to put down a greater load of bombs or, second, one can increase the accuracy of the bombing so that less of the bombs are 'wasted'. In fact, quite small improvements in bombing accuracy will greatly increase effectiveness.

The standard prewar German horizontal bombsight, the Goerz Visier 219, was a crude and ineffective instrument which gave poor results. To knock out pin-point targets with horizontal bombers using such a sight, large numbers of bombs would have to be released. On the other hand the Ju 87 dive bomber – a type which had been proved in action in Spain – had demonstrated an impressive ability to strike with great accuracy.

So it was that there grew up in the Luftwaffe an enthusiastic following for the idea of a long-range dive bomber. So far as the four and a half-ton short-range Ju 87B was concerned, the precision dive attack theory was sound enough. But when it came to be applied to larger aircraft, necessary if the diving attacks were to be carried out at longer ranges, the Germans began to run into trouble.

The first of the long-range dive bombers was the Ju 88, which was delayed considerably by the need to strengthen the airframe for this task. It weighed just over ten tons, over twice as much as the Ju 87, and was much more difficult to handle during the diving attack. In retrospect it is clear that the Ju 88 marked the upper limit of what was feasible in size and weight for a diving bomber. But the adherents to this type, notable amongst whom were Jeschonnek and Udet, pressed its development still further.

In 1938 and 1939 the third generation of German medium and heavy bombers, the fifteen-ton Dornier 217 and the thirty-ton Heinkel 177, reached the flight test stage. Half way through their construction it had been decided that they too would have to be strengthened for diving attacks. The early flight trials soon proved that both types were quite unsuitable for this purpose: in each case the severe stresses encountered during the pull-out from the dive proved to be too fierce for the airframe to stand as a regular service manoeuvre. In the event it was to be possible to use the Do 217 as a horizontal bomber, and it was capable of serving successfully in that role untroubled by its dive bomber origins. Not so the He 177. In the case of this four-engined bomber the motors were coupled together in pairs, each pair of engines driving a single airscrew. The conventional engine layout, under which each motor drove its own airscrew, would have resulted in an aircraft which was uncontrollable in a dive, and for this reason the coupled-engine arrangement was retained on the He 177 long after it should have been abandoned. Because of cooling and lubrication problems, as well as fuel spillage, the coupled motors displayed a discomforting tendency to burst into flames, and many He 177s were lost to these causes. As a result there were to be severe delays in the introduction of the He 177 into operational service.

One other important German replacement type was to suffer because of the need to be able to dive: the Messerschmitt 210, a combined heavy fighter, fighter-bomber and dive bomber, which was intended to replace both the Messerschmitt 110 and the Ju 87 then in service. This type was to prove an almost complete failure, because it had to be able to fulfil too many differing requirements for it to be able to meet any one of them satisfactorily.

The troubles with the replacement aircraft were not generally apparent in September 1939, however, for not until 1941 or 1942, if the war lasted that long, would such types be ready for large-scale service and necessary to replace those in use. In the meantime the Luftwaffe was about to face its first real test. Few people doubted that this newest air force, upon which so much effort had been lavished, would prove to be a formidable arm in war. And so it proved.

Messerschmitt Me 109F. The lack of wing armament was partly offset by a cleaner design — note absence of tail struts

The lightning victories

Hitler inspects men of the Luftwaffe involved in the capture of the Belgian Fort Eben Emael.

The Second World War opened early on the morning of 1st September 1939, when German troops stormed into Poland. During the morning, fog effectively prevented large scale air operations, but by the early afternoon it cleared and the Luftwaffe was heavily committed. The Germans had collected nearly 1,600 combat aircraft for the campaign, most of them concentrated in *Luftflotten I* and *IV*. Initially the main targets were the Polish airfields, and these came under continuous air attack from horizontal and dive bombers, and also strafing fighters. Those Polish pilots who did manage to get off the ground to intercept the raiders found their out-dated PZL fighters no match for the modern Messerschmitts which pounced on them.

With a total first-line strength at the beginning of the conflict of only only 397 aircraft, of which 159 were fighters and 154 bombers, the Polish air force could do little to influence events, and within two days the Luftwaffe had established almost complete air supremacy over their country. Thus relieved of their first responsibility, the German air commanders could move quickly on to their second: the support of the advancing ground forces. All Polish troop movements observed came under systematic attack from the air, and road and rail communications in the rear areas were repeatedly and heavily attacked. As a result the movement of Polish forces into and out of the battle areas was sometimes rendered completely impossible. Meanwhile continuous attacks on the retreating Polish troops by dive bombers greatly assisted the German soldiers by knocking out strong points, artillery batteries and troop concentrations.

General Kutrzeba, the commander of the Polish Army of Poznan, had this to say about the effectiveness of the German air strikes on his troops: 'Every movement, every troop concentration, and all march routes were taken under annihilating fire from the air . . . It was Hell come to Earth. The bridges were destroyed, the fords were blocked, the anti-aircraft and part of the other artillery forces were annihilated . . . Continuation of the battle would have been nothing but a matter of holding out, and to have remained in position would have posed the imminent threat that the German air force would have turned the whole place into a graveyard, since anti-aircraft defences in any form were completely lacking.'

By 17th September the Polish army was no longer able to operate as a co-ordinated fighting force, and for the Germans the end of the campaign was in sight. The fall of the capital, Warsaw, seemed imminent. Now the first German units began to move back, to buttress the weak forces facing the British and the French in the west. But because of a sudden stiffening of Polish resistance the capture of Warsaw proved to be much more difficult than had been expected. Following an unsuccessful propaganda and leaflet campaign the Germans launched a powerful air and artillery bombardment on the city on 25th September. The Luftwaffe commander responsible for the air attacks, General von Richthofen, committed some 400 bombers, many of which flew repeat sorties that day. From a camouflaged command post outside the city a satisfied Hitler watched the orgy of destruction; when night fell the Polish capital blazed from end to end. On the following day the forces defending Warsaw gave up the hopeless and one-sided struggle which was causing the loss of so many lives, and offered their surrender. The day after that, 27th September, the campaign in Poland came to an end.

Luftwaffe losses had been extremely light during this first action, considering what had been achieved. A total of 413 aircrew were killed or missing, and a further 126 had been wounded. Two hundred and eighty-five aircraft were lost and 279 damaged; of the former seventy-nine were fighters, seventy-eight horizontal bombers and thirty-one dive bombers.

Over Poland the Junkers 87 dive bombers proved to be an outstanding success, a success exploited to the full by the German propagandists. With hardly any opposition either from the air or from the ground to hamper them, the pilots had been able to make the most of the very high inherent accuracy of the steep diving

attack. To enemy ground troops utterly unprepared for it, the effect of this almost individual form of combat was devastating on morale. The Stuka legend, born in Spain, was confirmed as a terrifying reality.

After their victorious campaign over Poland the Luftwaffe combat units pulled back to their rear bases in Germany, to rest and refit. For both the Germans and their British and French adversaries this was a time for waiting quietly, and preparing for the battles that 1940 would bring. Aptly, the period was known at the time as the 'phoney war'.

While the troops on the ground faced each other along the static Western Front, the planning staffs were far from idle. For the Germans the main effort of the new year was to be a co-ordinated offensive into Holland, Belgium and France, which was to open in the late spring. But first Hitler insisted upon the capture of Denmark and Norway in order to secure his northern flank and as he put it, 'anticipate English action

During the early campaigns the Stuka legend was born

against Scandinavia and the Baltic.'

On 9th April 1940, without warning, the Germans struck out at unsuspecting Denmark and Norway – both of them neutral countries at that time. While armoured forces made an almost unopposed advance into Denmark, and ships of the German navy landed troops on the Danish islands and at Oslo, Kristiansand, Bergen, Trondheim and Narvik in Norway, German parachute troops made the first ever assault landing on the two airfields at Aalborg. Soon the town of Aalborg, as well as almost the whole of Copenhagen, was in German hands. Before the day had ended the Danish king and government could see that any further resistance to the invaders would result only in a futile loss of life, and the order was given to cease fire.

Meanwhile, the seaborne landings at the Norwegian ports had been synchronised with air attacks on the airfields used by the Norwegian air force; this small force was almost anihilated on the ground. Following this the airfields at Stavanger/Sola and Oslo/Fornebu were quickly captured by airborne troops, and became advanced bases for the dive bombers and twin-engined fighters flying missions in support of the German ground troops.

During the invasion of Norway the Germans made full use of their fleet of transport aircraft to fly in troops and Luftwaffe ground personnel; some 500 Junkers 52s were available for the operation, one third of them from the regular transport units and the rest on loan from the advanced flying training schools. The ability to rush in forces in this way played an important part in the rapid establishment of the German lodgement area in the south of Norway.

When the first British and French troops landed in Norway, at Narvik, Namsos and Andalsnes, on 15th, 16th and 17th April respectively, the Germans had secured a firm foothold in the south. Now the Luftwaffe struck hard at the Allied landing points, and at shipping bringing in supplies and reinforcements. Both level bomber and dive bombers maintained a constant pressure and, in the absence of any real air opposition, they were able to do considerable damage.

Meanwhile the German air build-up in Norway continued, and at the beginning of May 1940 *Fliegerkorps X*, the major unit committed, consisted of 710 aircraft.

LEVEL BOMBERS	360
DIVE BOMBERS	50
SINGLE-ENGINED FIGHTERS	50
TWIN-ENGINED FIGHTERS	70
RECONNAISSANCE AIRCRAFT	60
COASTAL TYPES	120

In the face of such strong air opposition, the Royal Air Force was unable to intervene effectively. Attempts to set up fighter bases were invariably observed by German reconnaissance aircraft, and then the landing grounds were bombed until they were useless.

On the ground the Germans continued relentlessly northwards up

the length of Norway, and in the early part of May the Allied troops had to be evacuated from Andalsnes and Namsos in the centre of the country. On 10th June the remaining forces, at Narvik in the north, were also withdrawn. The Germans were now in possession of the whole of the country.

From the beginning until the end, the Luftwaffe was an important factor in the success of the campaign in Norway. As we have seen, the seizure of the airfields at Oslo and Stavanger was made possible by the use of paratroops and air-landed units. And once these had been secured, bombers and long-range fighters operating from them were able to delay seriously the movement

The Bf 110 long range fighters were an outstanding success over Norway, where airfields were few

of British and French troops into the country. Later, when the ground battle developed, the command of the air proved to be a tremendous and often decisive advantage in a country where communications in the hinterland were poor and often consisted of a single road or railway line running through a valley between two towering mountains. But even before the two-month long battle for Norway had ended, the Germans had aimed their mighty thrust deep into France itself.

The planned German thrust into France in the summer of 1940 represented a calculated risk. In place of the small pincer movements which had proved so effective during the campaign in Poland, the German army now decided to drive a powerful armoured wedge, more than 200-miles long, between the northern and the southern groups of armies defending France; once the wedge reached the Channel coast and the two groups were severed from each other, they could be finished off one at a time. The thrust was a calculated risk because it would succeed only if the armed forces on the ground could maintain their momentum; if the tanks were ever separated from their supporting infantry and their supplies, then it would be the Germans who would find themselves in trouble.

Now the bombers of the Luftwaffe were really going to get the chance to prove what they could do. If they could bring powerful and concentrated

Above: A Dornier 17 releases its bombs. *Below:* Luftwaffe paratroopers jump from a Junkers 52 transport aircraft

air support to bear on obstacles in the path of the ground thrust, a sort of moving artillery barrage, there was a good chance that the gamble might come off.

However, before the opening phase of the advance into France, the Germans felt it necessary, as in the case of Norway and Denmark, to secure their northern flank by invading two hitherto neutral countries, in this case Holland and Belgium. As before, speed of movement was vital, so that the Germans could pierce the main Dutch and Belgian defensive lines before British and French help could become effective. To smooth the path of their advancing armoured troops, the Germans planned to use their airborne troops once again (but on a far larger scale than in Norway and Denmark), to seize vital bridges before they could be demolished by the defenders.

There was one further problem the Germans had to solve before they could open their attack: the capture or neutralisation of Fort Eben Emael. The main Belgian defence line, which was based on the River Meuse and the Albert Canal, hinged on the junction of these two water barriers. And it was at this junction that the Belgians had built an impressively strong fortified position, Fort Eben Emael, whose 75mm and 120mm guns threatened to dominate the entire area, To over come this obstacle the Luftwaffe had reserved a secret weapon which was now to be used in action for the first time – glider-borne assault commandos, which were to be landed *inside* the compound of the fortress itself.

During the offensive in the west the role of the Luftwaffe was to fall into three main parts. Firstly, it was to neutralise the opposing air forces by means of powerful bomber attacks on their airfields and fighter attacks on those aircraft which did get into the air. Secondly, it was to fly the airborne troops to their objectives. Thirdly, it was to smash a path for the armies invading Holland and Belgium and, later, the great armoured thrust into France itself. To support these ambitious plans, the force had available more than 4,000 aircraft.

LEVEL BOMBERS	1,300
DIVE BOMBERS	380
SINGLE-ENGINED FIGHTERS	860
TWIN-ENGINED FIGHTERS	350
RECONNAISSANCE	640
TRANSPORT AIRCRAFT	475
ASSAULT GLIDERS	45

The German offensive began early on the morning of 10th May 1940, with the planned bomber attacks on airfields in Northern France, Holland and Belgium. As a result of these the Dutch and Belgian air forces were virtually knocked out of the battle, while the British and French air forces in Northern France were seriously weakened: thus the Germans seized the initiative in the air at the very beginning of the battle.

Meanwhile, the troop transports and gliders had put down their loads under cover of darkness, and on the ground a series of fierce small-scale actions was being fought as the German airborne troops endeavoured to hold on to their objectives until the relieving tanks arrived. The three main airfields at The Hague were taken in quick succession, together with the vital Moerdijk bridge near Rotterdam.

The operation to take fort Eben Emael was a brilliant success. The assaulting force of eighty-five men in eleven gliders had set out just before dawn. Two of the gliders had become detached from their towing aircraft on the way but, ignorant of this, the remainder carried on and landed in the compound of the fortress. Exploiting the element of surprise to the full, the Germans sprang straight into action. Armed with specially prepared demolition charges, the carefully-briefed attackers set about the task of dealing with the heavily protected gun turrets. Where the turrets proved too strong or difficult to get at, two-pound charges of explosive on the gun barrels were sufficient to knock out the weapons. For the most part trapped below ground, the 750-strong Belgian garrison could do little to hinder the work of destruction going on above. Eventually German ground forces arrived to reinforce the glider-borne troops, and the bewildered defenders surrendered. German losses were six killed and fifteen wounded, while losses to the almost ten-times stronger Belgian garrison were twenty-three dead and fifty-nine wounded. There can be few more graphic illustrations of the value of surprise as a weapon of war.

With the major obstacles in their path cleared for them, the German armoured units plunged deep into Holland and Belgium. In the skies above, the aircraft of the Luftwaffe made full use of its virtually undisputed command of the air, to ensure that the defenders were allowed no breathing space. On 15th May, following a heavy air attack on the city port of Rotterdam in which 900 people were killed and a large part of the centre was gutted by fire, the Dutch government surrendered. By now, too, the Belgians were in grave difficulties. But already the centre of gravity of the battle had shifted to the south, for the Germans had opened their main offensive against France itself.

Punctually at 1600 hours on the afternoon of 13th May, the first wave of aircraft – Ju 87 dive bombers – had arrived over the west bank of the River Meuse, to begin the 'softening up' of the French positions there. Manning the uncompleted fortifications was the French X Corps, a formation made up of so-called 'B-class' soldiers – for the most part elderly reservists: the Sedan area was regarded as a 'safe sector' by the French High Command. Once again the screaming bombs from the diving aircraft shattered the morale of the men on the ground. As one French general later wrote:

'The gunners stopped firing and went to ground. The infantry cowered in their trenches, dazed by the crash of bombs and the shriek of the dive-bombers; they had not developed the instinctive reaction of running to their anti-aircraft guns and firing back. Their only concern was to keep their heads well down.'

With the French artillery smashed and the infantrymen cowering, dazed, in their trenches, General Heinz Guderian's *1st Panzer Division* was able to secure a bridgehead on the west bank of the river with only light casualties. German army engineers quickly assembled a pontoon bridge, and the first tanks rumbled across. By nightfall Guderian's men had seized the Marféy Heights, having smashed through both the main and the secondary defensive positions to get there.

On the 14th the German pontoon bridges over the Meuse near Sedan were the key to the invasion of France, and both sides saw this. That day the RAF Advanced Air Striking Force sent in every available light and medium bomber, and the French air force a similar striking force, with orders to wreck the bridges at all costs. All fighters that could be spared were sent to escort the raiders. But at the target the German fighter and flak defences were ready, and in the ferocious air battle which followed the French striking force was almost wiped out and the British lost forty out of the seventy-one bombers committed. The pontoon bridges remained standing.

The failure of the Allied air and ground counterattacks proved to be the decisive turning point in the Battle of France. With sufficient tanks across the Meuse the German armoured thrust began its push for the coast, and once it was under way there was nothing the British or French could do to stop it. While the Luftwaffe kept the Allied airfields under bombardment, strong formations of its dive-bombers prepared the way for the tanks. As soon as air or ground reconnaissance reports were received of points of resistance holding up, or likely to hold up, the armoured thrust, the Luftwaffe struck. By flying as many as nine

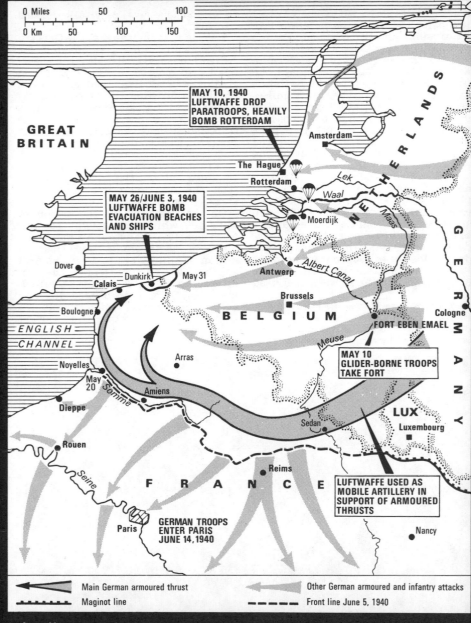

Scale:
0 Miles 50 100
0 Km 50 100 150

GREAT BRITAIN

NETHERLANDS

GERMANY

MAY 10, 1940 LUFTWAFFE DROP PARATROOPS, HEAVILY BOMB ROTTERDAM

Amsterdam

The Hague

Rotterdam

Lek

Waal

Moerdijk

Maas

MAY 26/JUNE 3, 1940 LUFTWAFFE BOMB EVACUATION BEACHES AND SHIPS

Albert Canal

Antwerp

Dover

Dunkirk   May 31

Calais

Boulogne

Brussels

BELGIUM

Cologne

FORT EBEN EMAEL

ENGLISH CHANNEL

Noyelles

May 20

Somme

Arras

Meuse

MAY 10 GLIDER-BORNE TROOPS TAKE FORT

Dieppe

Amiens

LUX

Rouen

Sedan

Luxembourg

LUFTWAFFE USED AS MOBILE ARTILLERY IN SUPPORT OF ARMOURED THRUSTS

Seine

Reims

F R A N C E

Paris

GERMAN TROOPS ENTER PARIS JUNE 14, 1940

Nancy

Main German armoured thrust

Maginot line

Other German armoured and infantry attacks

Front line June 5, 1940

Luftwaffe support for the Panzers

sorties per day with their dive-bombers, the Germans succeeded in paralysing all British and French attempts to check the advance.

By 18th May the main German armoured spearhead had reached the upper Somme, and two days later, after covering a further sixty miles, reached the sea at Noyelles. The daring German plan had succeeded: the northern and the southern groups of Allied armies had been severed apart. It was the beginning of the end of the Battle of France.

The very speed of the German advance presented some difficult supply problems, especially for the short range units of the Luftwaffe: the single-engined fighter, dive-bomber and reconnaissance units, in particular, were moving their bases almost daily. Most of the loads were brought in by road, but the versatile Ju 52s of the transport force were also used

Below: The wreck of an RAF Hurricane fighter, shot down in France.
Below right: The tail of this Ju 87 was damaged by anti-aircraft fire

to speed the arrival of vitally needed cargoes.

Having reached the sea, the German tanks swung north, to envelop the Allied troops. By 24th May the spearhead had passed Arras, had taken Boulogne and had reached Calais; at the same time the German army group which had advanced westwards through Belgium was maintaining its own, somewhat slower, movement forward. The position of the British and French troops cut off in the north of France was rapidly becoming untenable and on the evening of the 26th the first men were evacuated through the port of Dunkirk.

On the German side the armoured divisions which had fought so well were nearly exhausted, as more and more of their tanks were lost in action or simply broke down. As well as this, Hitler now feared that an all-out tank attack on Dunkirk might easily become bogged down in the marshy ground which surrounded the port. At this same time Göring was demanding that his Luftwaffe should be allowed to finish off the

enemy troops in a series of large-scale air attacks. Accepting the latter's promise that the Luftwaffe could do this, and in preference to risking the precious armoured divisions over unfavourable terrain, Hitler ordered the army to stop its advance twelve miles short of Dunkirk. Now it was up to the Luftwaffe.

Göring concentrated a force of some 500 fighters and 300 bombers against the shrinking Allied pocket, and the shipping off the shore. On paper the force was impressively strong, but the bomber and fighter units were also operating after two weeks of intensive action; the wear and tear had been considerable, and few could now go into action with anything like their full strength. Moreover, the German formations nearing Dunkirk often found themselves under attack from British fighters operating from bases in Southern England; unless close fighter cover was available, the bombers, and especially the dive-bombers, suffered heavy losses. For the first time the Luftwaffe was meeting in action an air force with equally high training and morale, and similarly modern equipment, in the air and in force. The German air attacks caused a lot of casualties amongst Allied ground troops, and sank many of the ships engaged in ferrying the survivors back to England. But they did not stop the evacuation. When the last vessel pulled away from the beach at Dunkirk, on the morning of 4th June, a total of 338,226 men had been snatched to safety.

Once the Dunkirk evacuation was over, the main body of the Luftwaffe was able to turn its attention to the support of the ground forces thrusting towards Paris. On 14th June the French capital fell, and eleven days later the French government sued for peace. The campaign in the west was over, just forty-six breathtaking days after it had begun.

Now only one of the opponents remained – Great Britain. And once the invincible German armed forces concentrated their attack there who could doubt that she, too, would soon be overcome?

First setback: the Battle of Britain

It was the loss of trained crewmen that made the Battle of Britain such a serious setback for the Luftwaffe

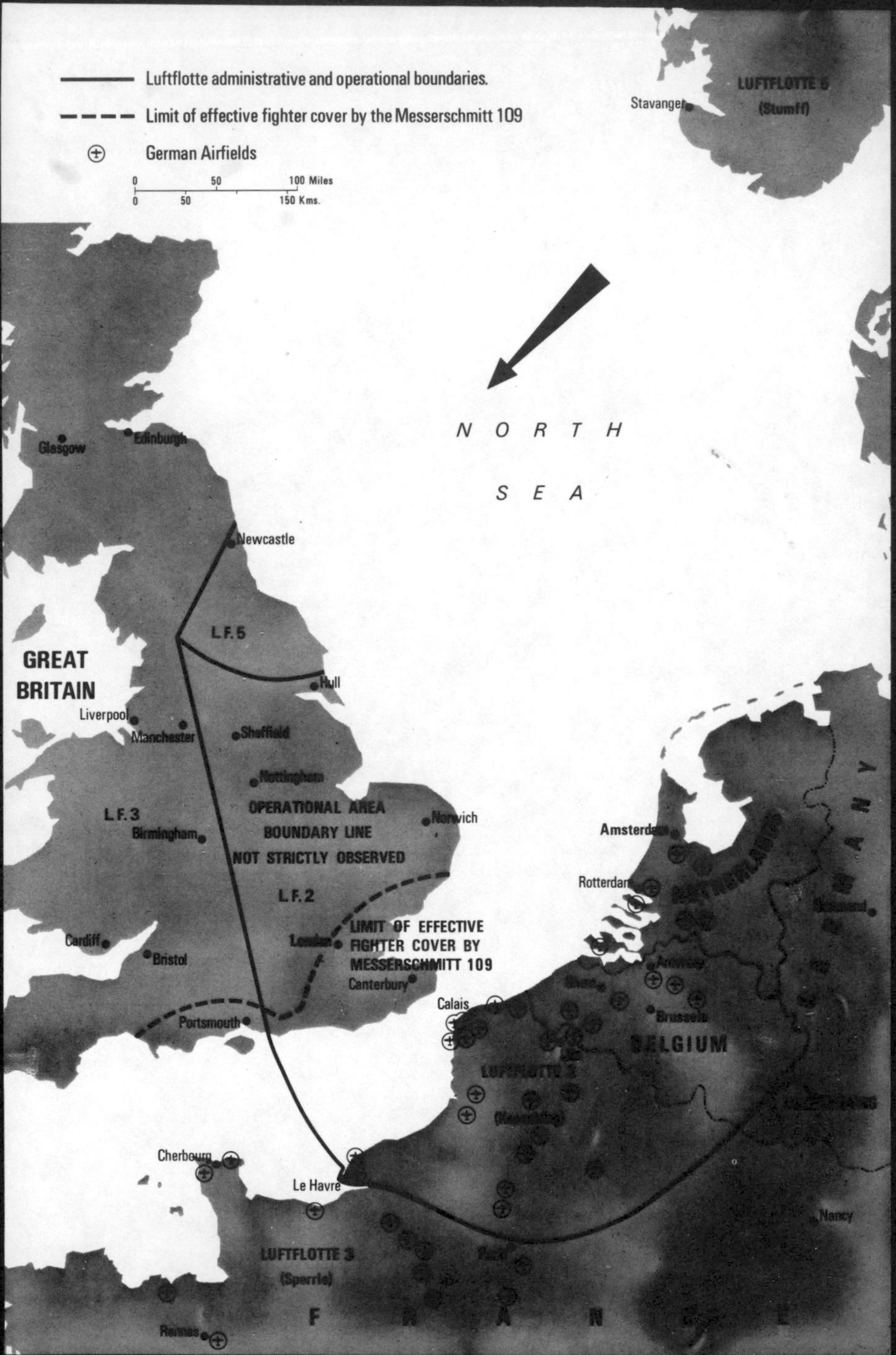

Luftflotte administrative and operational boundaries.

Limit of effective fighter cover by the Messerschmitt 109

German Airfields

0   50   100 Miles
0   50   150 Kms.

LUFTFLOTTE 5
(Stumff)

Stavanger

N O R T H

S E A

Glasgow Edinburgh

GREAT
BRITAIN

Newcastle

L.F. 5

Hull

Liverpool

Manchester

Sheffield

Nottingham

L.F. 3

Birmingham

Norwich

Amsterdam

OPERATIONAL AREA
BOUNDARY LINE
NOT STRICTLY OBSERVED

Rotterdam

NETHERLANDS

G
E
R
M
A
N
Y

L. F. 2

Cardiff

Bristol

London

LIMIT OF EFFECTIVE
FIGHTER COVER BY
MESSERSCHMITT 109

Canterbury

Antwerp

Portsmouth

Calais

Ghent

Brussels

BELGIUM

LUXEMBOURG

LUFTFLOTTE 2
(Kesselring)

Cherbourg

Le Havre

Nancy

LUFTFLOTTE 3
(Sperrle)

Paris

Reims

F   R   A   N   C   E

When the German army began planning for the invasion of Britain it is hardly surprising that the matter was treated in the same manner as the forcing of the Meuse, but on a larger scale. Both operations involved the crossing of a water barrier; it was only a question of degree. Just as before, the dive-bombers could take the place of the artillery to keep the defenders' heads down. But first, the Luftwaffe would have to have command of the air over the battle area. Göring was prepared to accept that it might take longer to annihilate the Royal Air Force, the most powerful air arm yet encountered, than the couple of days which had been sufficient for the others in Europe – the task might even take as long as two weeks.

During July 1940 more and more fighter and bomber units joined *Luftflotten II* and *III* positioned on the Channel coast, and by the 17th of the month the two *Luftflotten* could put up 2,600 aircraft.

LEVEL BOMBERS	1,200
DIVE BOMBERS	280
SINGLE-ENGINED FIGHTERS	760
TWIN-ENGINED FIGHTERS	220
RECONNAISSANCE AIRCRAFT	140

In addition there was *Luftflotten V* in Norway, which could put up 190 aircraft.

LEVEL BOMBERS	130
TWIN-ENGINED FIGHTERS	30
RECONNAISSANCE AIRCRAFT	30

During the planned operations against Britain the primary tasks of the Luftwaffe were the elimination of the Royal Air Force as an effective fighting force, and the strangulation of the nation's vital overseas trade by attacks on ports and shipping.

The Germans opened their attack in the middle of July, with light probing attacks and minelaying sorties. It was during one of the latter that Hauptmann Hajo Herrmann, the commander of the *7th Staffel* of *Kampfgeschwader 30*, and four of his crews took off from Zwischenahn in western Germany on the evening of 22nd July. Each of the Ju 88 bombers carried two 1,100-pound magnetic mines, intended for Plymouth Sound.

Dropping sea mines from the air was an exacting task. They had to be released when the aircraft was flying at less than 185 mph, or the parachute was liable to tear and the delicate mechanism of the mine would be damaged as it hit the water. It was also important to lay the mine accurately in shallow water and in used channels, since those landing elsewhere would be wasted; this need for accuracy imposed a maximum release height of 300 feet, because if they were released any higher the wind could carry the parachute and its load well clear.

Prior to the take off Herrmann and his men had studied the target carefully. They had decided to approach the Sound from the north-eastern, landward, side at their cruising altitude of 16,000 feet. Over Plymouth itself they would do a let-down to 300 feet, let go of their mines in the Western Channel and escape out to sea to the south west.

Herrmann arrived at the target area on time, and observed the coastline and the port itself in the light of the half-full moon. Out of sight in the darkness, the rest of his crews followed. The German pilot lined himself up over the north-eastern outskirts of Plymouth, heading south-west. Then he throttled back, and extended his under-wing dive breaks while at the same time trimming the aircraft nose-up. In this way he made the Junkers assume a flat, almost stalled, condition, as it descended silently and under control at an angle of forty-five degrees. By using these tactics Herrmann hoped that he would be able to retain the element of surprise, while at the same time he held the Western Channel in sight as he made his run in.

Suddenly, half-way down his descent, Herrmann was horrified to see a large sausage-shaped object silhouetted in the moonlight right in front of him: a barrage balloon. Instinctively the German pilot threw his bomber into a turn, but to no avail. The Junkers was flying very slowly, and the controls were sloppy and ineffective. The next thing Herrmann knew, he had collided with the balloon. Perhaps 'collided with' is not the right expression; because of the steep flat descent, it might be more accurate to say that the bomber had 'landed on top of' the balloon.

For the Germans in the aircraft it was a most frightening experience. The balloon was filled with highly inflammable hydrogen gas at low pressure; it had plenty of 'give' and withstood the force of the impact, killing off the bomber's speed in the process. Now both the balloon and its unaccustomed burden were falling rapidly.

'It lasted only for a few seconds, though it felt like an hour,' Herrmann later recalled. 'Then I noticed that the British searchlights were shining from above – we had 'fallen off' the balloon and now we were upside down, with virtually no forward speed, and going down out of control. I felt as though I was playing piano which was falling from a fifty storey building!' Herrmann slammed the dive brakes shut and selected full throttle, but still the controls would not 'bite'. There seemed to be no alternative but to abandon the plummeting bomber, and the pilot shouted to his crew to bail out. There was a blast of cold air as the escape hatch, comprising the rear half of the cockpit canopy, fell away. Then, at almost that same instant, the controls began to take effect and the Junkers levelled itself out a few hundred feet above the city of Plymouth. It was just as well for the German crewmen, for none of them had had time to get out.

In spite of the glare from a searchlight which had been following his antics, Herrmann could make out the breakwater right ahead. He was now, as he puts it, 'in the cage', flying low and slowly, heading right into the heavily defended port area which had been fully alerted, and coned by searchlights into the bargain. There was nothing for Herrmann to do but grit his teeth, hold his throttles wide open, and run the gauntlet. As he reached the breakwater he let go of the mines. From all sides strings of brightly-coloured tracer chased after the twisting bomber, but the Junkers bore a charmed life and there were no hits.

Once he was clear of the defences Herrmann turned his aircraft on to an easterly heading, and after a rather cold two hour flight he made an uneventful landing at Soesterberg in Holland. The Junkers 88 was surprisingly little the worse for its harsh treatment: both of the dive brakes were bent and the paint had been scuffed off the leading edge of the wings, but that was all. The fact that the propellers were neither marked nor bent suggests that they had not come into contact with the balloon fabric.

Small-scale operations like the one above and anti-shipping strikes continued until 13th August, Göring's

Adler Tag, when the action now known as the Battle of Britain opened in earnest. On that day the Luftwaffe put up 485 bomber and 1,000 fighter sorties during large scale attacks on Portland and Southampton, and also on airfields in Hampshire and Kent. These actions cost the Germans forty-five aircraft, the RAF thirteen. Two days later the Luftwaffe attacked in still greater force: with 1,266 fighter and 520 bomber sorties, it made a determined effort to smash the British fighter bases. The Royal Air Force reacted vigorously, and shot down seventy-five of the attackers for the loss of thirty-four fighters. The Germans tried the same thing again on the 16th, and lost sixteen aircraft, and yet again two days later when they lost seventy-one.

The pace of operations continued throughout the remaining part of August and early September. Then, at the end of the first week in September, following a series of attacks by the RAF on Berlin, Göring ordered that London was to become the primary target for his bombers. Now the aim was to break the morale of the British people.

On the afternoon of the 7th a force of 372 bombers, escorted by 642 fighters, set out to attack the British capital. Because the British fighter controllers had disposed the inter-

Above left: **Two ace Luftwaffe fighter pilots; left, Adolf Galland, and right, Molders. In the centre is Udet.** *Right:* **Otto von Ballasko**

ceptors in anticipation of yet another attack on the airfields, most of the bombers were able to reach the target without being molested, though some German units were badly knocked about during the return flight. The London dock area was hit particularly hard, and clouds of dense black smoke rose from an oil storage tank compound which had been set on fire. That evening Göring gleefully reported that 'London is in flames' and that in this 'historic hour' his Luftwaffe had 'for the first time delivered its stroke right into the enemy's heart.' Nevertheless, a follow-up attack two days later met with the usual strong fighter opposition and cost the Germans twenty-eight aircraft.

By now the realisation was permeating through the ranks of the Luftwaffe, from the bottom to the top, that this was one battle that the Germans were not going to win easily – if, indeed, they were going to win it at all. What had gone wrong? The fact was that the Luftwaffe, always victorious until now, had bitten off rather more than it could comfortably chew.

Above left: Bomber crewmen await the order to take off. *Far left:* Rear cockpit of a Do 17, showing one of the extra beam machine guns fitted when the British fighters became troublesome. *Left:* During high level attacks, oxygen masks were worn. *Above:* The Bf 110 was a failure as an escort fighter over Britain

To smash RAF Fighter Command as an effective fighting force the Germans had either to lure the British fighters into the air and destroy them there, or else bomb the fighter airfields and destroy them on the ground. But it soon became clear that the ill-armed German bombers were unable to fend off determined attacks with their own machine guns, so they were able to penetrate to their targets only under cover of a strong fighter escort; the German escorting fighters, then, were to destroy the British fighters as they rose to intercept. But it soon became equally clear that the large twin-engined Bf 110 long-range fighters were no match in a dogfight for the smaller and more nimble single-engined Spitfires and Hurricanes. So the brunt of the work of escorting the German bombers fell to the single-engined Bf 109, the only German fighter then available which could meet the British fighters on equal terms.

The result was that the whole battle hinged on the effective fighting range of the Bf 109 – a machine which then lacked the droppable extra fuel tanks which were later to become a feature of almost all fighters. Like its British counterparts this was a short range interceptor with a radius of action of about 125 miles. It was thus able to provide fighter cover only as far as London from bases in the Calais area, or to a little past Portsmouth from airfields in the Cherbourg area.

The escorts had to accompany the bombers from the French coast to the target, and back at least as far as the Channel. Since the Bf 109 could only barely cover the distance to London and back, with the necessary fuel margin for combat, the whole formation of bombers and escort fighters had to fly more or less in a straight line from the French coast to the target, and then straight back. This inflexibility of routing greatly eased the work of the British defences. Indeed, the whole question of providing escorts for the bombers remained a thorny problem for the Germans throughout the battle. After it had assembled into formation, each fighter *Gruppe* was supposed to pick up its bombers as they crossed the coast of France. But because radio communications between the fighters and the bombers were very poor, this linking up was often a difficult matter. Day after day several separate formations of bombers, one following closely behind the other, would each have to be met by their allocated fighter escorts, all within a few minutes and within a breadth of a few miles of coastline. There was little margin for error, and if things went wrong some of the fighter *Gruppen* would link up with the wrong formation of bombers; then some of the bombers would get double their share of protecting fighters, while others went without. Unescorted bomber formations over England usually suffered heavy losses.

By pulling most of his fighter squadrons back to airfields outside the range of the Bf 109 the British commander, Air Chief Marshal Dowding, made the policy of air attacks on his bases a costly proposition for the Germans. Moreover, the number of Bf 109s available during the battle was roughly the same as the number of Spitfires and Hurricanes available to the British; the latter had to be spread to cover the whole of the country while the single-engined German fighters were concentrated in the south, but this meant that the Luftwaffe had nothing like the superiority in numbers of single-engined fighters necessary in view of their other disadvantages.

The climax of the large-scale attacks on the British capital came on 15th September, with two separate raids by escorted bombers. That in the morning was met by twenty-four squadrons of Spitfires and Hurricanes, of which twenty-two engaged; the afternoon attack was engaged by all thirty-one of the British fighter squadrons sent up against it. The result was a series of hard-fought actions all over the southern part of England. And fighters were not the only hazard the German crews had to face. Leutnant Otto von Ballasko

flew a Heinkel 111 that day, and he recalls:

'So far as I was concerned, 15th September was bad from the very start. My own *Gruppe*, *III/KG 1*, was not operating that day, but I was to fill a space in a formation made up of aircraft from another *Gruppe*. Naturally, when that happens, they do not give you the best position. I was placed right at the rear of the formation and on the inside – just about the most difficult position of all to fly. At 20,000 feet our heavily laden Heinkels were very sluggish on the controls, and it required a lot of hard work to keep in place.'

The bombers flew from Cap Gris Nez near Calais straight to their target – Tilbury Docks, London. As the formation crossed the coast of England the formation closed up until the aircraft were flying just a few yards apart; now the Germans were as ready as they would ever be for the inevitable British fighter attacks.

Suddenly, as it was over the Royal Navy base at Chatham on the Thames Estuary, Ballasko's aircraft shuddered. It had been hit by anti-aircraft fire. Shell splinters sliced through the rudder control linkage, others peppered the starboard engine, which ground to a stop. The Heinkel immediately curved down out of the formation, and was soon left behind, alone.

After some rather hurried experimenting Ballasko found that things were not quite so bad as they had seemed: he found that it was possible to get some sort of directional control by rotating the rudder trimming wheel, which used a separate system of wires:

'By firing some red distress flares we managed to summon down a couple of Messerschmitts, and these now reassuringly formated on us. When we were hit we were within ten miles of our target, so we continued on and dropped our bombs there. This done, I had to turn the aircraft round for home. With only the rudder trimmer working it took a long time to swing the aircraft round, and in the process we found ourselves involuntarily drifting right over London itself! We were very lucky not to be hit yet again by the powerful flak defences.'

Shortly afterwards the guardian fighters began to run short of fuel. Their pilots pulled in close to the wounded Heinkel, waved good-bye and good luck, and disappeared southwards. Now the bomber crewmen were entirely alone over England, in broad daylight, in an aircraft which would not steer properly and which had only one engine working. And the nearest friendly territory was seventy miles away. The men could see the British fighters heading in all directions, but they seemed to be interested only in the great battles going on high above, and nobody bothered the lame Heinkel.

Clearly safety lay in keeping low, and trying to sneak out unobserved, so Ballasko eased the nose of his aircraft down to pick up speed and lose height. He crossed the entire length of Kent at low altitude, then the English Channel. Once back over France the German pilot set his bomber down in a field; all the crewmen got out without injury.

That day the Luftwaffe lost a total of sixty aircraft. The action marked the last of the really big daylight attacks on London to get through in force, and from then on German activity over Britain in the daytime began to taper off.

From then on, too, the Germans began to make more and more use of fighter-bombers, Bf 109s with a single 550-pound bomb fitted under the fuselage, or Bf 110s with two 550-pound and four 110-pound bombs, to attack London. Each *Gruppe* of fighter-bombers was provided with an escort of one *Gruppe* of fighters. Sometimes the escorting *Gruppe*, which flew high above the tight fighter-bomber formation, had a *Staffel* of its own carrying bombs. Then, if the main fighter-bomber force was attacked by British fighters, and the escorts dived to the rescue, the remaining fighter-bomber *Staffel* which had been flying with the escort would continue on to the target. This ruse worked on several occasions.

German fighter pilots play Skat and read as they wait near their aircraft for the order to scramble

Top: German bombers in the Battle of Britain attacked in close formation, but their combined fire-power was insufficient to ward off the British fighters. *Above and below:* Towards the end of the battle the Luftwaffe attacked London with bomb-carrying Bf 109 fighters

Typical of the fighter-bomber attacks on London was that on 15th October, when thirty Messerschmitts struck at the city at 9 am in the morning and scored some hits on Waterloo station. Three quarters of an hour later came a second wave, this time of fifty fighter-bombers, which dropped bombs near Tower Bridge. At 11.30 am yet another formation of Messerschmitts attacked the capital. During their approach flights the German aircraft would run in at heights of up to 33,000 feet, where they presented the British defences with an extremely difficult interception problem. Consequently there were few large dogfights, and losses on both sides were comparatively light during this phase.

But the fighter-bombers could carry few bombs and, because of the inherent difficulty of accurate bombing from high level in such aircraft, those they did drop were usually scattered over a wide area and failed to cause any concentration of damage. These were little more than nuisance raids.

The battle to knock out the Royal Air Force was over, and the British fighter pilots were as active as ever. During its attempt, from 10th July to 31st October, the Luftwaffe had lost 1,733 aircraft to destroy 915 British fighters. In truth, from the beginning of October, the raiding Messerschmitts served merely as a token German presence over London during the daylight; the main bomb-attacks were now being made under cover of darkness, when the British defences were far less effective.

The night bombing attacks had begun back in August, when on 28th of the month and on the next two nights strong forces of German bombers had attacked Liverpool. Then, on 7th September, the so-called night *Blitz* on London had opened; between that date and 13th November the Germans had bombed the British capital almost on every night, with a raiding force averaging 130 aircraft.

During these large-scale night attacks the German crews would have liked to have used their highly-developed *Knickebein* beams to find their targets. The *Knickebein* (bent leg) system employed powerful ground beam transmitters – there were eleven of these in France, Germany, Holland and Norway positioned to throw their guiding beams over England. The radio operator in the German bomber was able to pick up the *Knickebein* signals on a simple receiver; if he heard dots or dashes he knew he was to one side or the other of the beam, but if he heard a steady note he knew he was in the centre of the beam. The Germans would use two separate *Knickebein* transmitters to mark a target, one to guide the aircraft during their approach to the target, and the other to cross the first at the target so that the crews knew when they had reached the bomb release point. *Knickebein* was a simple device, usable by all German twin-engined bombers. It *could* have guided the bombers to the British cities with considerable accuracy. But, fortunately for the British people, it was never really given the chance to prove its worth.

To test out their beam system operationally, the German crews had made use of *Knickebein* during the light probing attacks in July and early August – operations like Herrmann's minelaying sortie to Plymouth Sound. In the course of these small-scale actions the Germans picked up a lot of useful information on the operational value of the device. But so did the British Intelligence service, which quickly deduced the deep significance and the peril represented by the dots and dashes in the ether. On direct orders from Mr Churchill, the Royal Air Force formed a special organisation to jam *Knickebein*. The method was simple enough: powerful British ground transmitters radioed dash signals on the German beam frequencies. On the dash side of his beam the German aircrewmen heard the real and the British dashes; as the aircraft flew through the centre of the beam they heard the German steady note signal together with the British dashes; on the dots side of the German beam the men heard dots and dashes which fell into no recognisable pattern. After much hard work the British jamming organisation was ready by the middle of August – just in time to combat the heavy Germany night raids which began at the end of the

month. It had indeed been a close run thing. The German bomber crews quickly discovered that now that they really needed it, *Knickebein* was useless over England; now the mass of the bombers was without an accurate means of target-finding over enemy territory, and as a result the accuracy of the night bombing was poor.

Thus thwarted in their original design, the Germans tried another tack. One unit, *Kampfgruppe 100* (flying Heinkel 111s), was equipped with an improved radio beam system codenamed *X-Gerät;* the *X-Gerät* was much more complicated than *Knickebein* and could be used only by highly trained crews, but it was very accurate indeed. The idea now evolved was that *Kampfgruppe 100* should arrive over the target first and light it up with accurately placed incendiary bombs, then the rest of the 'de-Knickebeined' attacking force could drop their bombs on the marker-fires.

Kampfgruppe 100 first operated in its new role of a pathfinder on the night of 14th November 1940; the target – Coventry. Once the *X-Gerät*

aircraft had started marker-fires round the aiming points, German bombers headed in towards the city from all directions. One 'crocodile' of attacking aircraft flew in over the Wash, another over the Isle of Wight, and a third over Brighton. Each of the German units had its own specific target to destroy. For example: *I/LG 1* was briefed to attack the works of the Standard Motor Company and the Coventry Radiator and Press Company; *II/KG 27* the Alvis zero engine works; *I/KG 51* the British Piston-Ring Company; *II/KG 55* the Daimler Works; and *KGr 606* the gas-holders in Hill Street. Most of these objectives suffered serious damage. Altogether 449 bombers hit Coventry during the ten hours of the attack, and between them they dropped fifty-six tons of incendiaries, 394 tons of high explosive bombs and 127 parachute mines. As a result a large part of the centre of the city was left in ruins and twenty-one important factories, twelve of them concerned with aircraft production, were badly hit. Five hundred and fifty people were killed, and a further

800 suffered wounds. It was a striking demonstration of what the Luftwaffe was capable of, when its radio beam systems were free of interference.

But already the British Intelligence service was hot on the trail of the *X-Gerät*, and suitable equipment to jam out its beams was in production. When the Germans tried to repeat the Coventry success, against Birmingham on 19th November, the Royal Air Force was ready. *Kampfgruppe 100* found considerable difficulty in finding the city, and ended up by starting a few small and scattered fires to the south of it. When the main force of bombers arrived, they wandered aimlessly round for some time before finally unloading their cargoes over a wide area. The attack was a failure, as was a similar one on the same target the following night.

During the months that followed, *Kampfgruppe 100* led many attacks, but because of the steadily growing barrage of jamming put out by the Royal Air Force the success at Coventry was never repeated. Towards the end of 1940 the Germans introduced yet one more gadget to help path-

Above: **The Germans came at night.**
Far left: **One of their most successful attacks was on Coventry, in 1940**

finder aircraft reach their targets, the *Y-Gerät*. But again the British found out about it, and jammed that as well.

Even when they attacked targets which lacked proper jamming cover, the Germans still had to contend with the decoy fire sites (code-named 'Starfish') ignited by the British to mislead them. Major Victor von Lossberg commanded the *Y-Gerät* pathfinder unit *III/KG 26* during the attack on Liverpool on the night of 3rd May 1941. He recalls that during his approach to the target he led his *Gruppe* in as high as possible, at around 22,000 feet, in order to get the greatest possible range from the Y-beam transmitter situated near Cherbourg. Each of his Heinkels trailed a pair of long white condensation trails behind it, which looked rather like railway lines silhouetted against the moon. Then Lossberg's throat dried as he saw one of the pairs of lines begin to twist and curve, then disappear altogether: British night fighters were active. The beam signals ended some seven minutes flying time short of the city, near the small town of Wrexham, but he continued on to Liverpool on dead reckoning. Suddenly, below him, in a position he knew from his bombing equipment to be well short of Liverpool, Lossberg observed fires blazing up on the ground. Yet no bombs had fallen. In fact this was the decoy 'Liverpool', built ten miles to the south of the city on the mouth of the river Dee. The pathfinders went on to release their incendiaries accurately, but as they headed south afterwards they were helpless spectators as they watched bomber after bomber in the follow-up force release its load on the decoy. That night *III/KG 100* lost three of its aircraft, testimony to the steady improvement to Britain's night defences during the spring of 1941.

During the whole time of the day and night attacks on Britain one German unit, *I/KG 40*, had waged, almost single handed, a campaign against shipping in the Atlantic. Operating from Bordeaux/Merignac in France and Stavanger/Sola and Trondheim/Vaernes in Norway, the unit's long-range four-engined Focke Wulf 200 Kondors had shuttled back and forth round the western seaboard of the British Isles, attacking any ships they came across.

The period from August 1940 to July 1941 was one of great opportunity for the men of *I/KG 40*. As one of the Kondor pilots, Hauptmann Bernhard Jope, now recalls: 'The convoys, even quite large ones, often sailed with hardly any air defences at all. On the Kondor we could carry only a few bombs, but we could go in very low when attacking the ships, and make every one count.' And the German pilots would certainly attack at low level. They would run in to bomb at about one hundred feet above the waves, pulling up after they had released their bombs only to clear the ship's masts. Using tactics such as these *I/KG 40* sank eighty-eight ships totalling 390,000 tons during January, February and March 1941. These figures are all the more remarkable when it is considered that only rarely were more than eight of the Kondors serviceable at any one time.

For the Germans it was all too good to last, and of course it did not. The ships began to carry increasingly powerful anti-aircraft batteries. And, following the 'Destroyers for Bases' deal between Britain and the USA, under which fifty old USN destroyers were transfered to the Royal Navy in exchange for the right to use bases in the British West Indies, more escorts became available to protect the convoys.

The net result was that from the spring of 1941 the Kondors' low altitude attacks on the shipping became increasingly risky. Now, if they were not to suffer severe losses, the German crews were able to attack only if they had a measure of surprise. The big bombers would stalk the convoys, dodging from cloud to cloud then, when conditions were judged favourable, they would sweep in fast and somewhat higher than before and attack the first ship that happened to be in front of them; there was no question of a leisurely picking of the fattest target, as in the past. The aircraft would make one hasty bombing run, then try to make its escape before the fireworks began. Once the element of surprise was lost, there was no question of a second bombing run, for that would be little short of suicide. Obviously, such hastily executed attacks were much less effective than the earlier ones had been, but in spite of these new measures the German losses began to mount alarmingly.

Now the real limitations of the Focke Wulf Kondor began to manifest themselves. For the fact was that while this aircraft – a converted civil airliner – could dish out the punishment, it could not take it. The frail structure and the mass of extra fuel tanks for the long-range role both meant that the aircraft was not able

to withstand much in the way of battle damage.

During the early part of 1941, first in a trickle and then, in May, a flood, the bulk of the Luftwaffe – with the exception of a few combat units, notably *Kampfgeschwader 40* with its Kondors and two *Jagdgeschwader* left in France – moved east in preparation for the attack on Russia. The force was scheduled to return to France to renew the attack upon Britain about six weeks after the beginning of the offensive in the east – Hitler's estimate of how long he expected the Russians to be able to hold out. In the event, when the bombers did return to France, it was as only a shadow of their former strength.

So ended the three-phased attack calculated to knock Britain out of the war. First, there had been the attempt to wipe out the Royal Air Force and so leave the nation defenceless to attack from the air. Then when that failed the Germans had tried by break the will of the British people by day (the second phase) and night (the third phase) attacks on centres of population. That failed too. And the whole time the Luftwaffe and the steadily expanding U-boat arm strove to sever Britain's umbilical chord – the shipping which brought in her vitally needed foodstuffs, raw materials, and armaments from the USA and the Empire. The British had taken the measure of the Kondors; it was to take somewhat longer to master the U-boat threat but this, too, was done.

To what extent can the Battle of Britain be considered to be a turning point of the war? Certainly it did not mark the beginning of the end of the Luftwaffe, for that force continued in being and was still to achieve triumphs as great as any it had gained during the first year of the war. But what was significant was that for the first time the main body of the Luftwaffe had been committed and had failed; the force was trained and equipped as a tactical air arm, and when it was used as a strategic weapon it was almost bound to fail. And in the process it suffered severe losses in aircraft and – far worse – trained men. The myth of the invincibility of the Luftwaffe had been exploded for ever.

In the Balkans
and the
Mediterranean

The Luftwaffe's move eastwards had begun in January 1941, and by March about 400 German combat aircraft had collected in Rumania in preparation for the planned attack on Greece. The Germans had taken it for granted that the Yugoslavs would fall in with their plans, and their surprise was all the greater when, in March a *coup d'état* ousted the pro-German government there. Hitler decided that he would have to occupy Yugoslavia as well as Greece, in order to secure his southern flank prior to the offensive in Russia.

To reinforce *Luftflotte IV* in the Balkans, for the added responsibility of providing air cover during the attack on Yugoslavia, a further 600 aircraft were transfered to it from the west. That such a large force could move into bases 1,000 miles away from those previously occupied in France, and fly into action at one half of its established strength within ten days of the order to move, illustrates once again the impressive mobility of the Luftwaffe. The force had received a black-eye from the Royal Air Force over Britain, but it was still more than a match for any of the other air forces in Europe.

On Palm Sunday, 6th April, the Germans struck. The air assault on Yugoslavia opened with a powerful bombing attack early that morning on the capital, Belgrade. A force of 150 level and dive bombers, with strong fighter escort, easily knocked out the weak fighter and gun defences, then set about the business of destroying Belgrade unmolested. The result was a catastrophe for the Yugoslav capital: when the attack on the ill-prepared city closed, 17,000 people lay dead in its ruins. Having delivered its knock-out blow on the opposing air force and the capital, the Luftwaffe could shift its attention to the more usual targets in support of the army: troop concentrations, lines of communication and targets in the actual battle area. As before, the combination of concentrated air support and powerful armoured thrusts on the ground proved unstoppable, and twelve days after the campaign opened the Yugoslavs surrendered.

The simultaneous attack on Greece was equally successful. On the very first evening, Ju 88s of *KG 30* attacked the country's largest port, at Piraeus near Athens. A lucky bomb struck the ammunition ship *Clan Frazer* which was tied up to one of the quays for unloading; the resultant explosion, as the 250 tons of explosives in her holds were set off, wrecked the Greek port from end to end. At one stroke this deprived the British and Greek forces of the one really well equipped harbour through which supplies could pass.

With the usual close support from the Luftwaffe, the German ground forces advanced swiftly through Greece, and within two days had entered Salonika. One by one the defensive lines in the mountains were turned, and soon it was clear that the Allied position was rapidly becoming untenable. On 24th April, while British troops were fighting a drawn-out action to delay the Germans, the first men of the expeditionary force were evacuated by sea. Three days later the invaders entered Athens, and on the 28th April – just over three weeks after the campaign had started – the last of the British forces left on the mainland of Greece surrendered. The German machinery of *Blitzkreig* – lightning war – was working as smoothly as ever.

Even before the final capture of Greece, the German planners were considering the last objective in the limited Balkans campaign: the strategically placed island of Crete, sixty miles to the south of the mainland of Greece. On 25th April Hitler signed his twenty-eighth war directive, which stated:

'As a base for air warfare against Great Britain in the Eastern Mediterranean we must prepare to occupy the island of Crete (Operation Mercury)... Command of this operation is entrusted to the Commander-in-Chief of Luftwaffe who will employ for the purpose, primarily, the airborne forces and the air forces stationed in the Mediterranean area . . . ' Unlike those of other nations, which invariably belonged to the army, the German airborne troops were an integral part of the air force. Hence the Luftwaffe responsibility for the attack on Crete.

For the airborne invasion a force of

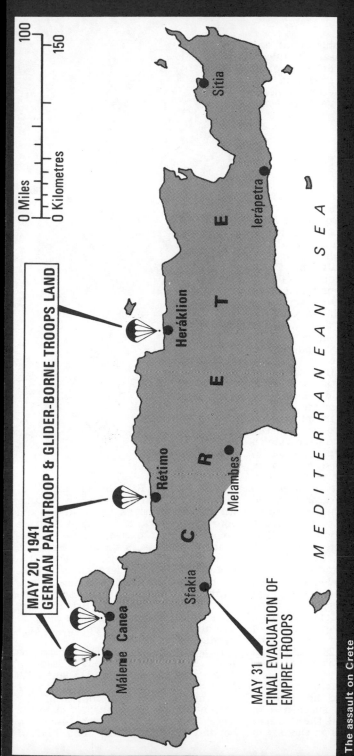

MAY 20, 1941
GERMAN PARATROOP & GLIDER-BORNE TROOPS LAND

Máleme   Canea

Sfakia

Rétimo

Heráklion

Melambes

Ierápetra

Sitia

C R E T E

MEDITERRANEAN SEA

MAY 31
FINAL EVACUATION OF
EMPIRE TROOPS

0 Miles   100
0 Kilometres   150

The assault on Crete

493 Ju 52 transports, plus about one hundred DFS 230 assault gliders, collected at the airfields around Athens. The task of providing the necessary air support fell to General Freiherr von Richthofen's *Fliegerkorps VIII*, which comprised 650 aircraft.

LEVEL BOMBERS	280
DIVE BOMBERS	150
SINGLE-ENGINED FIGHTERS	90
TWIN-ENGINED FIGHTERS	90
RECONNAISSANCE AIRCRAFT	40

It took the Germans only four days to eliminate the weak British aerial opposition, and by 18th May the Luftwaffe had full control of the skies over Crete. Now the bombers began systematic 'softening up' operations against the ground defences.

The airborne assault on Crete opened early on the morning of 20th May, preceeded by an hour of intensive air attacks on the defences round the dropping zones. Then the Ju 52 transports arrived, and the first waves of paratroops and gliders descended on Máleme, Caneá, Rétémo and Heráklion; in each case the first of the landings were synchronised with the end of the bombing attacks, so that the German troops could take advantage of the newly created bomb craters for cover. But in spite of all this the airborne troops suffered heavy losses at first, and were able to make little headway. Only gradually, and with the fullest use of the powerful air supporting forces available, were the Germans able to prise the British, New Zealand, Australian and Greek troops out of their positions. For the invaders the turning point came late on the afternoon of the 21st, when they finally managed to secure the airfield at Máleme. Even though the runway was still under artillery fire, scores of Ju 52s landed with fresh troops as well as sorely needed supplies; meanwhile *Fliegerkorps VIII* effectively stopped the defenders from receiving worthwhile quantities of supplies. Things got worse for the Allied forces, and on 28th May the Royal Navy began to evacuate men from the island.

During the ground battle for Crete the Royal Navy, defying the threat of the dive bombers, had succeeded in turning back almost all the German attempts to land troops on the island

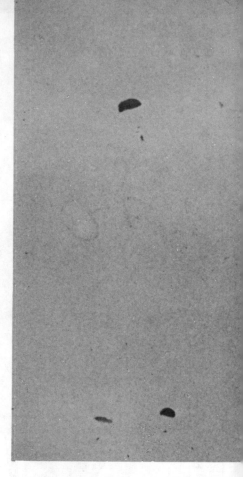

by sea. But von Richthofen's force had reacted violently, and in the ensuing air-sea battles sank two cruisers and four destroyers, and caused damage to an aircraft carrier, three battleships, four cruisers and one destroyer. Now the emphasis shifted to the withdrawal of the defenders, and at a cost of one cruiser and two destroyers sunk, and three cruisers and three destroyers damaged, the British ships took off 16,000 men before the remainder on the island were forced to surrender on 1st June.

But the German airborne troops had also suffered serious losses. Of 13,000 paratroops engaged, about 4,500 had been killed or were listed as missing. During the course of the action 272 of the transport aircraft were destroyed or else damaged beyond repair – more than half of

those committed. As Generaloberst Student, the commander of the German airborne forces, put it, Crete was 'the grave of the German paratroops'. Never again were the Germans to mount a large scale airborne assault, and these highly trained troops fought out the rest of the war as infantrymen.

Since the beginning of the war in the Mediterranean the small British-held island of Malta, fifty-six miles to the south of Sicily, had been a thorn in the Axis side. During February and March 1941 General Hans Geisler's *Fliegerkorps X*, plus a few units from the Italian Air Force, had mounted heavy air attacks on the island, aimed primarily at Valetta harbour and the various airfields. Almost the whole of Geisler's bomber force, comprising 120 level and 150

A Junkers 52 transport goes down in flames, during the paratroop invasion of Crete

dive-bombers, was enaged in this task. At regular intervals they launched synchronised dive-bombing and low-level attacks using Ju 87s and Messerschmitt 110s, while Ju 88 and He 111 bombers with fighter escort undertook medium level bombing from 5,000-8,000 feet. Then, in April, the attacks began to taper off as the demands of the other fronts began to draw the Luftwaffe combat units away from Sicily.

During the spring of 1941 Hitler's eyes were firmly fixed on the main objective: Russia. Once the Bolshevik menace was out of the way the small fry like Malta could be dealt with at leisure.

Russia: the victorious drive eastward

The Germans, and Hitler in particular, had long regarded the Russians as a latent source of danger. And in spite of the non-aggression pact which existed between the two nations, there was little trust between them. The Russian advances westwards since 1939, when they had occupied the whole of Latvia, Estonia and Lithuania, and also parts of Poland, Rumania and Finland, served to confirm Hitler's belief that sooner or later Germany was bound to find herself at war with Russia.

Between 1939 and May 1941 the strength of the Russian army had increased from sixty-five to 158 divisions, and the majority of these were located along her western frontier. Ostensibly these forces were manning defensive positions; nevertheless, they were regarded in Germany as an implied threat. Also during this period, the Russian armed forces had been undergoing an extensive re-equipment programme, while the General Staff was at last recovering from the drastic thinning of its ranks suffered during Stalin's savage purge in 1938.

Whether or not the Russians really did intend to invade Germany will not be known for certain until the Soviet government archives of the period are opened to historians for publication. What matters is that Hitler *thought* that sooner or later they were going to attack, and thus resolved to get his blow in first.

It was at the end of July 1940, after the end of the campaign in France but well before the opening of the Battle of Britain, that Hitler had first ordered planning to begin for the attack on Russia. By the middle of November 1940 the operational planning staffs of the Luftwaffe had started on detailed studies. Meanwhile air force works units were engaged in bringing the relatively primitive airfields in occupied Poland up to German standards for all-weather operations.

At this time Göring tried his hardest to turn Hitler away from his chosen course. On one occasion the Luftwaffe commander is recorded as saying: 'My *Führer*, the ultimate decision is yours to make. May God guide you and help you to prove that you are correct in the face of this opposition! I, myself, am forced to oppose your viewpoint on this matter. May God protect you! But please remember that it will not be my fault if I cannot carry out our plans for the expansion of the Luftwaffe.' Hitler replied: 'You will be able to continue operations against England in six weeks.' Then Göring pointed out: 'The Luftwaffe is the only branch of the German armed forces that has not had a breathing space since the beginning of the war. I said at the beginning of the war that I was going into battle with my training units, and now they have all been used . . . I am not at all certain that you can defeat Russia in six weeks. The ground forces cannot fight any more without Luftwaffe support. They are always screaming for the Luftwaffe. There is nothing that I should like better than that you are proven right. But, frankly, I doubt that you will be.'

Göring's impassioned appeals were in vain; the *Führer* refused to be swayed. Had not a few brave but ill-equipped Finns come near to defeating the Russians during the Winter War of 1939?

At first the invasion of Russia was to have had the code-name '*Fritz*'; later this was changed to '*Barbarossa*', after the crusading Germanic Emperor Frederick Barbarossa. The attack was to have opened early in May 1941, but the unusually late thaw that year resulted in a 'mud season' which lasted until the end of that month. As a result the operation had to be put back to the third week in June. This loss of nearly six weeks was to have decisive consequences later.

In order to maintain secrecy regarding the German intentions, most of the flying units assigned to the *Barbarossa* operation were kept back in the occupied territories in the west or in Germany until the beginning of June 1941. Then, within a space of three weeks, the various *Gruppen* moved swiftly into the bases previously prepared for them. As soon as they landed the aircraft were

The most important Soviet aircraft production centres remained out of reach of the Luftwaffe bombers

Above: **Hs 123 ground-attack aircraft return to their base.** *Left:* **Aerial reconnaissance in Russia**

taxied to their dispersal areas, where they were carefully camouflaged.

When the German attack on Russia opened, shortly before dawn on the morning of 22nd June 1941, the strength of the Luftwaffe units engaged amounted to 2,770 aircraft.

LEVEL BOMBERS	775
DIVE BOMBERS	310
SINGLE-ENGINED FIGHTERS	830
TWIN-ENGINED FIGHTERS	90
RECONNAISSANCE	710
COASTAL TYPES	55

The great pains the Germans had taken to maintain secrecy paid handsome dividends during the initial phase of the operations, and the Russians were taken by complete surprise. As always, the initial target for the Luftwaffe during this campaign was the opposing air force, and the Russian airfields along her western border were subjected to intensive air attacks.

For their attacks on the Russian airfields the Germans used for the first time a new type of fragmentation bomb, the 4-pound SD 2. These small cylindrical weapons, three inches in diameter, three and a half inches long, were carried in large numbers in special containers fitted to the attacking aircraft; a Ju 88 or a Do 17 could carry 360 SD 2s, a Bf 109 or a Ju 87 up to ninety-six. After being released in rapid succession the bombs' casings opened up to form a pair of 'wings', and the individual weapons spun down to the ground rather like sycamore seeds. The bombs would scatter over the ground to cover a wide area, and the seven-ounce explosive charges would go off on impact. Against 'soft' targets like unprotected aircraft, these small shrapnel bombs proved to be very effective. Unhampered by the weak Russian defences, the Germans were able to make low-level attacks and plant the SD 2s accurately amongst the lines of parked aircraft.

The attacks on the airfields were successful beyond the wildest German dreams. Soviet combat aircraft were destroyed by the hundred as they sat out in the open in neat rows with no attempt at dispersal or concealment. The official Soviet postwar publication *History of the Great Patriotic War of the Soviet Union* records: 'During the first days of the war enemy bomber formations launched massive attacks on sixty-six airfields in the frontier region, above all on those where the new types of Soviet fighters were based. The result of these raids and the violent air-to-air battles was a loss to us, as at noon on 22nd June, of some 1,200 aircraft, including more than 800 destroyed on the ground.'

But while the material damage inflicted on the Soviet air force was to be crippling in the short term, the losses in trained manpower were only light. As a result the long-term recuperative powers of the Russians were hardly affected. Moreover, the lack of a suitable German long-range bomber meant that the important Russian aircraft factories situated near or beyond the Ural Mountains were beyond reach.

With the Soviet air force out of the battle the Luftwaffe could revert to its usual task of supporting the army. The tried and tested methods of concentrating all available bombing aircraft – level as well as dive-bombers – against enemy communications, troop concentrations and even close support targets, was repeated after the pattern established in Poland, France and the Balkans. As in the past, the rapid advance of the German army through Soviet-occupied Poland and western Russia demanded the greatest mobility on the part of the short-range fighter and dive-bomber units; once again the Luftwaffe transport organisation proved equal to the task.

One of the outstanding features of the early part of this campaign was the lavish use the Germans made of aerial reconnaissance. As we have seen, more than a quarter of the entire Luftwaffe force committed at the opening of the offensive comprised reconnaissance types. Thus the German army commanders were able to get detailed and up-to-date information on enemy dispositions and movements in the rear areas, and generally in the fighting areas as well. The main problem in the actual combat zone was that of identifying friend from foe. Sometimes this was very difficult, especially when the Russians learnt not to leave their vehicles and run for cover at the approach of German aircraft. Reconnaissance aircraft were often lost to ground fire when their pilots brought them down to low altitude an an attempt to positively identify ground troops below. When they could the German ground units would mark their forward positions with swastika flags and coloured fabric panels laid out on the ground. This system was backed up by an elaborate and changing system of using coloured smoke and flare signals. For their part the Russians tried very hard to imitate the German identification signals, and sometimes succeeded. On several occasions attacks on Soviet troop concentrations had to be called off because the German aircrews were unable to make a positive identification in time.

Sometimes the situation on the ground was such that risks had to be taken, and inevitably air strikes did hit friendly forces on occasions. For example, on 1st August Luftwaffe bombers struck at troops of the German *23rd Division* advancing on Kiev and caused 'serious losses'. As long as army commanders demand close air support for their men there will be, in spite of all precautions, losses to friendly troops at times.

But if the reconnaissance picture the Luftwaffe presented to the German High Command was sometimes patchy, it was incomparably better than that available to their Soviet opposite numbers. In a campaign where the rapid movement of armoured forces was the order of the day, this advantage often proved to be decisive.

Over half of the operational strength of the Luftwaffe was concentrated in Russia during the initial stages of the attack, but because of the great length of the front – more than 1,000 miles – it was impossible to be strong everywhere. As a result the short-range fighter, bomber and reconnaissance units had often to switch their positions from one part of the line to another, in order to concen-

Right: The burnt-out wreck of a Russian I-15 fighter. *Far right:* A sledge is used to carry bombs to a waiting Dornier 17

trate to support ground attacks wherever the army high command launched each successive offensive.

Throughout the summer and autumn of 1941 the Germans advanced deeper and deeper into Russia. In seven great encircling battles, at Minsk, Smolensk and Uman, at Gomel, Kiev, Vyasma and on the shores of the Sea of Azov, the Germans captured a total of two and a half million prisoners, more than 9,000 tanks and 16,000 guns. During these encircling operations the mouth of each pocket in turn was closed initially by only relatively weak German armoured formations, which had the difficult task of preventing the Russians from breaking out until the slower-moving German infantry divisions could get into position. At this time the Luftwaffe was able to play an important part by delaying the Russian attempts to break out, or to relieve their enveloped forces by means of attacks from outside. However, these spectacular victories were not always bought cheaply, and the German method of employing all types of bomber for close support work had its own disadvantages. The Russian troops did not 'go to

ground' on the appearance of enemy aircraft, but instead opened fire on them with almost any weapon which came to hand. Over a period this policy caused the Luftwaffe very serious losses: between the beginning of the campaign and 27th September 1941 – just over three months – 1,603 German aircraft were shot down and a further 1,028 were damaged. Thus the total number of aircraft destroyed or damaged during this time, 2,631, was almost equal to the number committed to the campaign at its beginning. The losses of the cheaper aircraft – the dive bombers and the army co-operation types – were bad enough, but the steady drain on the more expensive He 111s and Ju 88s was such that replacements no longer kept pace with losses. Moreover, since most of the aircraft lost were over Russian-held territory at the time, losses in trained aircrew were severe; these were to prove the most difficult of all to replace. Gradually the fighting strength of the Luftwaffe was bleeding away.

For Generaloberst Ernst Udet, the head of the Luftwaffe aircraft development and production organisation, the magnitude of the losses over

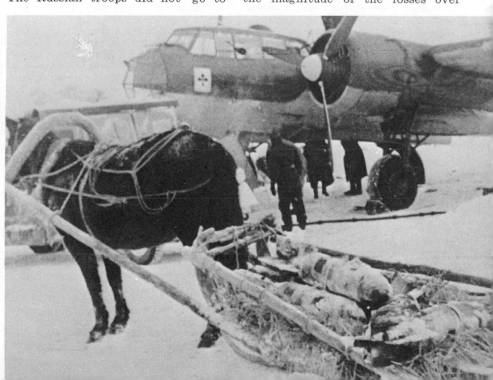

Russia proved to be the last straw. Throughout his tenure of this important office he had failed miserably to bring production up to the necessary levels; so long as the Luftwaffe maintained a strong reserve this was not so bad, but the heavy loss rates over Britain and then Russia changed all that. Moreover, the aircraft he had relied upon to replace the ageing He 111s, Ju 87s and Bf 110s, the He 177 bomber and the Me 210 fighter-bomber, were suffering serious teething troubles and both were close to failure. The mistakes made in the final two years of peace were now coming home to roost. The failure of Udet's work to keep the Luftwaffe properly equipped, both in quality and in quantity, was now becoming clear to all. Udet's health began to fail, and he suffered from haemorrhages and unbearable headaches. Finally, on the morning of 17th November 1941, he shot himself.

On Hitler's orders the circumstances of Udet's death were kept secret. That evening the German Information Bureau announced that: 'The General in charge of Luftwaffe supplies, Generaloberst Ernst Udet, was killed on Monday the 17th November 1941, testing a new weapon. He died of his injuries on the way to hospital. The *Führer* has ordered a state funeral for this officer who died in so tragic a manner while in the performance of his duty. In recognition of his magnificent achievements in the First World War, of his sixty-two fighter victories and of the great services he rendered in building up the Luftwaffe, the *Führer* has perpetuated Generaloberst Udet's name by bestowing it upon *Jagdgeschwader* 3.

Udet's successor was Erhard Milch, who thus regained the position he had lost in 1938. Milch immediately began the thorough overhaul of the whole German aircraft industry, to cut out wasteful duplication and the inefficient use of manpower and resources. But such measures would not have much effect on the equipment situation in the short term.

There is an old Ukrainian proverb that runs 'In the summer one bucketful of water will make one spoonful of mud; in the autumn one spoonful of water will make a bucketful of mud.' When the autumn rains came in October 1941 the German troops advancing into Russia learnt the truth of the proverb. Previously firm ground turned into a morass, roads were covered in deep, sticky, mud. Movements by motorised fighting and supply units became possible only with the greatest difficulty. When their armoured thrusts slithered to a halt in axle-deep mud, the Germans were at the gates of Moscow and had almost surrounded Leningrad; they were never to take either of these cities.

Now the Germans were to pay a high price for the lateness of the spring thaw earlier in the year. For the Russians' greatest ally, 'General Winter', struck soon after the autumn rains and before the Germans had gained the rapid and total victory so confidently predicted by Hitler. And, also in December 1941, the United States entered the war against Germany; this was to have far-reaching effects, but much later.

The severity of the Russian winter found the Luftwaffe ill-prepared. Apart from the lack of proper cold weather clothing, there was a sorely-felt lack of the equipment necessary to maintain aircraft under such conditions. Because the machines often had to be parked out in the open in temperatures as low as minus 20 F, aero engines and guns simply froze solid, and all manner of heating devices had to be improvised in the field to thaw them out.

Added to the unexpectedly harsh winter conditions and the heavy losses was the cumulative wear and tear of some of the most intensive air operations ever mounted. Most of the Luftwaffe combat units had been in action without a pause from June until the end of October. During this period the dive bomber *Gruppen* had maintained an average daily sortie rate of about seventy-five per cent of their establishment in aircraft, the fighters sixty per cent and the level bombers about forty per cent. Considering that this effort was kept up day in, day out, for more than four months, these figures are in each case quite remarkable; they go a long way towards explaining why the Luftwaffe was able to achieve so much during the initial stages of the Russian campaign.

By the end of 1941 the Luftwaffe had only about 1,700 aircraft of all types on the Eastern Front, thinly spread along the 2,000-mile long front which ran from the North Cape to the Black Sea. And, because of the difficulties of maintenance and supply, the serviceability in many of the already weakened flying units fell to as low as thirty per cent. The Germans desperately needed a short breathing space to recover from the previous months' exertions. But they were not to get one, for early in December the Red Army launched its winter counteroffensive.

In the face of attacks by fresh Russian divisions specially trained and equipped for winter fighting, the exhausted German troops began to give ground. The spectre of what had befallen Napoleon's Grand Army in 1812 hovered large and menacing. There can be little doubt that any German attempt to make a general withdrawal would have rapidly become a rout. In the face of this threat Hitler's order to stand firm, whatever the cost, was undoubtedly correct. By the end of February 1942 the Germans had largely succeeded, in the face of powerful Russian pressure, in establishing a new defensive line, albeit a line critically thin in places.

When the front finally stabilised two German strongholds had been isolated, one at Demyansk and a smaller one at Kholm. The Luftwaffe was given the task of supplying the troops from the air.

At Demyansk, a small town almost mid-way between Moscow and Leningrad, the Russians had cut off six divisions of the German *Sixteenth Army*, comprising about 100,000 men. The airlift opened on 20th February, when forty heavily laden Ju 52s flew into the pocket, unloaded, and returned filled with wounded. The two airfields in the besieged area, at Demyansk itself and at Peski, were such that operations were possible only during the hours of daylight. Indeed, Peski was strictly an emergency airfield with a runway of rolled snow, and was usable only by the most experienced pilots. From the air-field at Pleskau to the pocket was a distance of 150 miles, of which about one hundred were over Russian-controlled territory. But the Soviet air force, still smarting after the severe punishment it had received in the summer, was unable to intervene with any effect against the transport aircraft.

By requisitioning Ju 52s from every possible source, notably the flying training schools in Germany, the Luftwaffe managed to collect a force of nearly 600 aircraft for the airlift. The daily average requirement for the besieged units was 300 tons, and this figure was almost met. What had started off as a temporary expedient soon developed into a protracted operation, which lasted until the seige was lifted on 18th May.

The force surrounded at Kholm was far smaller than that at nearby Demyansk – there were only about 3,500 men – but the problems facing the Luftwaffe were more severe. In the first place there was no usable airfield within the pocket, and supplies had either to be dropped by parachute or else flown in by gliders. Two types of glider were employed, the DFS 230 with a one-ton capacity, and the Gotha 242 with a two-and-a-half-ton capacity; in either case the gliders could make only a single journey because there was no means of retrieving them from the pocket. The glider crews were used as infantry. The men at Kholm held out for three and a half months before they were relieved by German ground forces.

The airlift operations to the pockets at Demyansk and Kholm were the largest to be undertaken up to that time, and they cost the Germans nearly 300 aircraft, excluding the gliders. They were successful in holding ground and perhaps saving units which might otherwise have been lost. But, as we shall see, the greatest significance of the operations was that they created a very dangerous precedent.

The thaw set in in April 1942, and with the resulting mud season, air and ground activity on the Eastern Front came to a virtual halt. The Luftwaffe was at last able to get the breathing space it needed, to bring

The Ju 52 bore the brunt of the operations to air-supply cut-off German troops in Russia

its units up to establishment in both men and machines in preparation for the forthcoming summer campaign. The main thrust, the German High Command had decided, was to be concentrated in the south, with the objective of overrunning the important Russian oil-producing areas in the Caucasus.

But first the southern flank had to be secured, and that meant that the Germans had to occupy the remainder of the Crimea, and in particular the Russian fortress of Sebastopol. Accordingly, in May 1942, Luftwaffe units began to concentrate in southern Russia.

The attack on Sebastopol opened on 2nd June, and was almost unparalleled in its ferocity. On the only occasion during the Second World War, the siege of a modern fortress was pushed through to the final reduction. The Germans had brought up the most powerful siege train to be assembled during the war, which included mortars of up to 60cm (23.5-inches) calibre, and even an 80cm (31.5-inches) calibre gun which fired shells each weighing nearly five tons. Richthofen's *Fliegerkorps VIII* provided the air support; the unit had not gained its reputation as a hard-hitting force for nothing, and while the ground artillery pounded the defences, Richthofen's men were flying some of the most intensive bombing operations ever mounted. Operating from bases just ten minutes flying-time from the fortress, the aircraft made as many as eighteen sorties each day. A Ju 88 with full fuel tanks at the beginning might make four bombing sorties in quick succession before the crew climbed out to stretch their legs. In spite of the most stubborn resistance, the outnumbered and outgunned Russian defenders were gradually forced out of their positions, and on 3rd July the fortress fell.

With their southern flank secured by the capture of Sebastopol, the Germans were able to push ahead with their planned thrust towards the Caucasian oilfields. The offen-

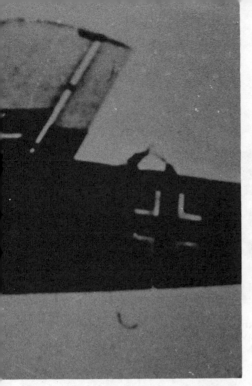

sive began at the end of June, and soon the German armoured formations were advancing down the line of the River Don. Throughout the rapid advance from Voronezh towards Stalingrad and into the Caucasus, a large part of the German level bomber force in the east was engaged in systematic operations against communications targets situated in the Russian rear areas. These extended over a wide area, and bridges, ferries and railways were all heavily attacked.

It is possible that had Tsaritsyn not been renamed Stalingrad in 1925, the industrial Centre on the River Volga would not have acted as a magnet for the two opposing armies in the summer of 1942. Certainly the city named after the Russian dictator was not so important, militarily, that it warranted a fight to the death between two major nations. But, whatever their reasons, it was here that both Hitler and Stalin chose to pit their all.

It was on 23rd August that leading elements of the German *Sixth Army* reached the Volga just to the north

of Stalingrad. The initial thrusts to seize the city were all repulsed, and in the face of a stiffening Soviet resistance the Germans were forced to fight hard for every house and every street. The bitterly fought contest dragged on through September and October, as both sides fed fresh divisions into the inferno; soon each of the opposing armies in this southern part of Russia comprised over a million men, and was supported by more than 1,000 aircraft. With incredible bravery and recklessness, German and Russian fought each other for possession of the city's rubble. With its usual intensive air support from the Luftwaffe, the *Sixth Army* moved deeper and deeper into the ruins. By the middle of November the Germans had secured almost the entire west bank of the Volga; the Russians could not now hold out much longer. Then the Red Army began its own counter-offensive outside the city.

On 19th November the reinforced Russian armies in position to the north of Stalingrad began their attack, to be followed on the next day by those in the south. They quickly sliced their way through the thinly stretched forces opposing them, and advanced to meet each other. Three days later, on the afternoon of 23rd November, the two claws of the pincer snapped shut. Locked in the pocket were twenty-two German divisions totalling 330,000 men. There is little doubt that at this stage the greater part of the trapped army could have fought its way through the cordon to safety, though with the loss of much of its heavy equipment, for the Russians had still to consolidate their gains. But Hitler was loath to pull back his men from the Volga. Instead he asked Göring whether or not the Luftwaffe could now supply the men of the *Sixth Army* surrounded at Stalingrad, just as it had at Demyansk earlier in the year; the latter replied that it was possible. The die was cast.

Acting on Göring's promise, Hitler ordered the commander of the forces beseiged at Stalingrad, Generaloberst Paulus, to hold the position. The garrison required an absolute minimum of 700 tons of supplies each day, or 500 tons if all the horses were slaugh-

Above: During the Stalingrad operation the Luftwaffe was combed for aircraft; these Ju 86s, obsolete bombers, were among the types used.
Below: When the airfields were captured, supplies were parachuted in

tered and their carcasses issued as part of the meat ration. To the air staff officers planning the airlift, it soon became clear that the Luftwaffe would have the greatest difficulty meeting even the 500 ton target; the maximum that could be promised was 300 tons per day.

The airlift began promptly on 25th November, but from the very start things went badly. The weather conditions were far worse than they had been during the Demyansk airlift, with periods of dense fog alternating with snow storms and just a few clear periods in between. Thus hindered, the airmen were able to deliver only sixty-five tons during the first two days and hardly anything at all on the third. Only on the sixth day of the airlift did the total flown in reach one hundred tons – one third of what the Luftwaffe had promised and one fifth of the trapped army's absolute minimum requirement.

To augment the regular Ju 52 transport units committed to the Stalingrad operation, the Luftwaffe was scoured for aircraft. At the beginning of December *Fliegerkorps VIII* of *Luftflotte III*, the unit responsible, was employing ten *Gruppen* of Ju 52s, two full *Geschwader* and two *Gruppen* of He 111 bombers operating in the transport role, two *Gruppen* of Ju 86s (out-dated bombers now being used

as transports), one *Gruppe* of He 177s, and a composite heavy transport *Gruppe* flying Fw 200s, Ju 90s and Ju 290s; in all, some 500 aircraft. Within a short time the addition of aircraft from the advanced flying training schools swelled this number to nearly 850. But in spite of this prodigious effort the Luftwaffe was never once able to fly in the daily target figure of 300 tons which it had set itself. The harsh flying weather, the hastily improvised airfields, the approach and return flights made over enemy-held territory in the face of increasingly strong Russian fighter and anti-aircraft interference and, later, the artillery bombardment of the airfields within the pocket, all these things combined to slow up the airlift. The net result was that the Luftwaffe was able to deliver to Stalingrad an average of only one hundred tons of supplies per day.

Short of the food, fuel and ammunition necessary to fight on effectively, the Germans in the Stalingrad pocket were forced to give ground. On 16th January 1943 the vitally important supply airfield at Pitomnik fell and after the loss of Gumrak airfield on the 22nd there was no airfield left to the surrounded troops which was suitable for a large scale airlift. The Germans were forced to resort to dropping the supplies in parachuted containers, a much less efficient method than that previously used because each aircraft was now able to fly in only about half the weight of ammunition or provisions on each sortie. For the *Sixth Army*, it was the beginning of the end. Weakened by hunger, the German soldiers were often unable to retrieve canisters which fell in the deep snow.

Now the issue could not be long in doubt, and on 24th January Paulus sent a signal to Hitler: 'Troops without ammunition or food . . . Effective

command no longer possible . . . 18,000 wounded without any supplies or dressing or drugs . . . Further defence senseless. Collapse inevitable. Army requests immediate permission to surrender in order to save lives of remaining troops.' Hitler's reply was immediate: 'Surrender is forbidden. The *Sixth Army* will hold their positions to the last man and the last round and by their heroic endurance will make an unforgettable contribution toward the establishment of a defensive front and the salvation of the Western World.'

But the dazed and broken men starving and freezing to death deep in Russia were beyond the exhortations of even the *Führer* himself, and on 2nd February 1943 the 91,000 survivors at Stalingrad finally surrendered.

The ill-considered attempt to keep the *Sixth Army* supplied from the air cost the Luftwaffe a total of 488 aircraft. Most of these losses were due to crashes while taking off and landing at the badly equipped Russian airfields in atrocious weather conditions, though towards the end of the airlift the Russian fighters did become increasingly active and exacted a heavy toll.

The long term effects of the exertions at Stalingrad were to cause serious problems in the Luftwaffe some time after the city had fallen. The losses in aircraft were bad enough, but in time these could made up. What was far worse was that the aircrew training programme back in Germany had been forced to grind to a halt when the aircraft and instructors were sent to Russia to take part in the airlift; losses in both were heavy. Moreover, the airlift had caused a serious shortage in high grade aviation fuel; this shortage had first become apparent in the late summer of 1942, but instead of the expected lull in operations during the time of the autumn rains to allow production to catch up, the need to support the attack on Stalingrad had resulted in intensified air operations. To prevent the shortage from getting worse the Germans were forced to cut back on all non-operational flying – and once again it was the training organisation which suffered. The resultant lowering of both the quality and the quantity of new aircrews, coming as it did after a time when losses had been high, was to cause great harm to the fighting ability of the Luftwaffe.

The spring thaw at Pitomnik airfield

The Junkers Ju 52

Originally designed as a single-engined transport, the Junkers 52 first flew In its three-motored form in 1932. Before the war the type saw world-wide service as an airliner, and it was ordered as a bomber/transport for the re-forming Luftwaffe. The Ju 52 did go into action as a bomber in Spain, but losses were uncomfortably high and it was rapidly replaced in this role. The type went on to become the standard transport type in the Luftwaffe, and continued in service until the end of the war; other Ju 52s were used as trainers, others still were modified to explode magnetic mines from the air. Production continued until 1944, and a total of 3,234 examples were built. *Specification of the Junkers Ju 52/3mg7e: Engines:* Three B.M.W. 132T motors, developing 830 hp for take off. *Armament:* One 13mm and two 7.9mm machine guns. *Load:* 18 fully equipped troops, or an equivalent freight load. *Maximum speed:* 189 mph. *Service Ceiling:* 18,000 feet. *Normal Range:* 930 miles. *Span:* 95 feet 10 inches. *Length:* 60 feet 8¼ inches

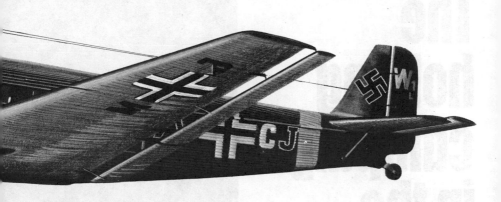

The Heinkel HE 177
Illustration shows the He 177A-O, the production prototype. The specification for the He 177A-5, the version produced in the greatest numbers, is as follows: *Engines:* two Daimler Benz DB 610 engines, each comprising two DB 605s; the coupled motor developed 2,950 hp at take off. *Armament:* varied from sub-type to sub-type, but typically it comprised up to 13,200 pounds of bombs, two 20mm cannon, three 13mm machine guns and four 7.9mm machine guns. Some versions of this bomber were modified to carry Fritz X and Hs 293 guided missiles.
Maximum speed: 303 mph at 20,000 feet. *Maximum range:* 3,400 miles carrying two Hs 293 missiles. *Service ceiling:* 26,250 feet. *Weights:* Empty 37,038 pounds; maximum loaded 68,343 pounds. *Span:* 103 feet 1¾ inches. *Length:* 66 feet 11¼ inches

The holding campaign in the west

The Heinkel He 177 did not, as shown by the death of its predecessor, fulfil expectations. Although it appeared on occasional sorties, its employment...

The Do 217 was one of the main types used during the Baedekker attacks on Britain

With the opening of the Russian campaign in June 1941, the Luftwaffe had concentrated the greater part of its striking power in the east. *Luftflotte III* in France retained only some 130 Ju 88s, Fw 200s and Do 217s, which engaged in anti-shipping and minelaying sorties aimed at disrupting Britain's trade. In addition there were two *Geschwader* of Bf 109s for air defence.

In Germany itself the main responsibility for the defence of industrial targets rested initially with the Luftwaffe flak units. Before the war the Germans had grossly over-rated the capability of their anti-aircraft guns, and after an inspection of units in the Ruhr, Göring had confidently stated on 9th August 1939: 'Above all, I have seen to it that the Ruhr, where the people must be able to work in peace, receives the greatest security. We will not expose it to even a single bomb from any aircraft.' During the course of the war this not entirely accurate prediction was to be emblazoned on scores of British and American bombers attacking the Reich.

As soon as the Royal Air Force began its night bombing attacks on Germany, in May 1940, it had become clear that the anti-aircraft guns alone would not be sufficient to curb the menace. So it came about that in July 1940 Oberst, shortly afterwards Generalmajor, Josepf Kammhuber received orders from Göring to build up a night fighter force to combat the British raiders.

At the end of 1940 Kammhuber's force comprised 165 aircraft, for the most part Bf 110s. At this time the German night interception tactics depended on searchlights to illuminate the bombers, which the night fighter pilots then attacked visually. This system was known as *Helle Nachtjagd* (illuminated night fighting), and using it the fighters did score a few victories. But the big disadvantage of the method was that the searchlights were all positioned near the cities, and this meant that the tactics rarely achieved anything outside the target areas. Moreover, there was the ever-present risk that the gunners would open fire on the fighters by mistake. To overcome these difficulties Kammhuber positioned his searchlights clear of the German cities, and therefore clear of the guns, in a belt which ran parallel to the coast, from Schleswig-Holstein in northern Germany to Liège in Belgium. The bombers were to be intercepted as they crossed this line on the way to their targets.

The linear system of defences using searchlights worked well enough on clear nights, but when there was more than one half cloud cover the night fighter pilots found it very difficult to make an interception. To overcome this problem the Germans introduced two types of radar, the *Freya* long-range early warning set and the *Würzburg* short range precision set, in order to assist the night fighter controllers on the ground in passing accurate information about the raiders to the men in the air. The ground radar stations were set up at twenty-mile intervals immediately in front of the searchlight belt, and Kammhuber encouraged his crews to attempt a radar-controlled interception first then, if this failed, they could follow the bomber into the searchlight zone and attack it there. The method of close radar-controlled interceptions bore the code-name *Himmelbett* (four-poster bed).

The German night fighter force expanded steadily during 1941, and by the end of that year it comprised some 300 aircraft. By now, with the availability of more and more equipment, the line of ground radar stations had lengthened considerably; it was shaped like a giant sickle: the 'handle' ran through Denmark from north to south, and the blade curved through northern Germany, Holland, Belgium and eastern France to the Swiss frontier.

Up till the beginning of 1942 Royal Air Force Bomber Command had been mainly concerned with its own expansion and re-equipment, and its attacks had been more of a nuisance than a threat to the Germans. All this ceased on the night of 28th March 1942, when a force of 234 bombers razed much of Lübeck in an extremely concentrated attack.

The Focke Wulf Kondor operated from Bordeaux/Merignac in France

The Lübeck raid aroused considerable resentment in Germany, and Hitler ordered the Luftwaffe to retaliate. On 14th April *Luftflotte III* units in the west were told: 'The *Führer* has ordered that the air war against England is to be given a more aggressive stamp. Accordingly when targets are being selected, preference is to be given to those where attacks are likely to have the greatest possible effect on civilian life. Besides ports and industry, terror attacks of a retaliatory nature are to be carried out against towns other than London. Minelaying is to be scaled down in favour of these raids.'

The first of the German attacks in the new series was mounted on the night of 23rd April when forty-five bombers, mostly Do 217s of *KG 2*, raided Exeter. This first attack was a failure but a second, on the following night on the same target with sixty aircraft, did cause heavy damage. On the third and fourth nights the target was Bath, which was also hit hard in the raids which together comprised 250 sorties.

But, even as the Germans were hitting Bath, the bombers of the Royal Air Force were systematically wrecking the German town of Rostock in a series of fire raids spread out over four separate nights. When Hitler heard what had happened, he was beside himself with rage. On 26th April he made an impassioned speech in which he shouted that he would take a copy of Baedecker's guidebook, and mark off the British cities one by one as they were destroyed; as a result the whole series of attacks became known in Britain as the 'Baedecker Raids.'

Following the attacks on Bath came others on Norwich and York. Then, after a rest of two days, the Luftwaffe returned to Exeter yet again on 3rd May. During this attack the German target marking was very accurate, and the bombers struck hard. Fierce fires quickly took hold of the heavily timbered mediaeval buildings and, unhindered by the narrow streets, raged unchecked until a large part of the city had been gutted.

For the remainder of May the Luftwaffe concentrated on the more lightly defended towns and cities, and hit Cowes. Hull, Poole and Grimsby. Then, on the last day of the month, the old cathedral town of Canterbury was raided.

The British defences in 1942 were considerably stronger than they had been the previous year, and they took a steady toll of the raiders. As a result the initial fervour of the 'Baedecker Raids' soon died away. The final spasm – three attacks on Birmingham and one on Hull at the end of July – cost the Luftwaffe twenty-seven bombers and caused little damage. The reader may get some idea of the cumulative effect of these losses from the fact that *Kampfgeschwader 2*, a Do 217 unit which had been deeply committed during the attacks on Britain throughout the first nine months of 1942, had lost aircraft and crews equal to its own strength once in each successive three month period. With the demands of the Russian front these losses were not all made good, and after starting 1942 with eighty-two crews the unit had only twenty-three left by September.

While *Luftflotte III* had been unable to maintain the momentum of its attack on Britain, Bomber Command of the Royal Air Force had gone from strength to strength. On 30th May a force of more than 1,000 bombers had hit Cologne, and caused serious fires and caused much damage. In recognition of the increasing effectiveness of Kammhuber's line of defences, the British bombers now began to fly to and from their targets in compact streams, in order to saturate the defences while the line was being crossed. Throughout the autumn and winter of 1942 the British attacks gained in weight, as more and more of the new four-engined bombers entered service. And Hermann Göring was forced to modify his 1939 prediction on the safety of the German cities; on 4th October 1942 he stated: 'I make every attempt humanly possible to prevent air attacks and ease the situation.'

A further disturbing development for the Germans, in August 1942, was the opening of the USAAF daylight bombing offensive. The threat built up gradually, for at first the B-17s did not go beyond peripheral targets in France, Holland and Belgium. As a result the German fighter pilots were given time to get used to their new adversaries – initially they had held the heavily armed B-17s in some awe, and were loath to press home their attacks to close range. But it soon became clear that the bombers' guns were not so effective as they had feared, and the fighter pilots soon regained their old aggressive spirit. At the same time Major Egon Meyer, the commander of *Jagdgeschwader 2*, equipped with both the Bf 109 and the new Focke Wulf 190, developed a method of attacking the B-17s from the front where their armament and their armour were less heavy; using these methods, his unit scored several victories.

At the end of 1942 the defences of Germany proper comprised nearly 400 night fighters and approximately 200 day fighters; the flak defences comprised 600 heavy batteries (88mm, 105mm and 128mm guns), 300 light batteries (20mm and 37mm guns), 200 search-light batteries and 40 batteries of balloons. Thus far, these defences had gained a healthy respect from the British, and sufficed for the time being to prevent the Americans penetrating deeply in daylight. But the attacking forces were gaining in both strength and experience with each month that passed, and there could be little doubt that 1943 would see hard-fought air battles over Germany itself.

Since the defeat at Stalingrad there had had to be a marked change in the outlook of the Luftwaffe High Command. Now it was clear that there would be no rapid victory in Russia, where the greater part of the force was tied up. But it was becoming equally clear that the Luftwaffe was ill-prepared for a long war. From the start the force had been designed for the high speed campaigns which had characterised the first three years of the war. Then the Germans had risked, and often accepted, high losses in order to achieve quick victory. And provided the victories came quickly, it did not matter so much if the advanced training organisation had had to be robbed of aircraft and instructors in order to reinforce the air transport force, if the war was going to be over before the new crews were really needed. The net result of all this was that at the beginning of 1943 the Luftwaffe faced a critical shortage of trained aircrew.

Coupled with the breakdown of the aircrew training programme was the general shortage of up-to-date combat types. In almost every case, the types in large scale use at the beginning of 1943 were developments of machines in service at the beginning of the war; the sole exception was the Focke Wulf 190 fighter. And, as we have seen, the two most important replacement types – the Heinkel 177 heavy bomber and the Messerschmitt 210 long-range fighter-bomber – had run into serious troubles which still had not been fully cured at this time. Because of this, the Luftwaffe had to order the aircraft industry to turn out still more of the ageing Bf 109s, Bf 110s, Ju 87s, Ju 88s and He 111s; the latest versions of the Bf 109 and

The German night fighter force took a steady toll of the RAF night raiders: Ju 88Cs of NJG 2

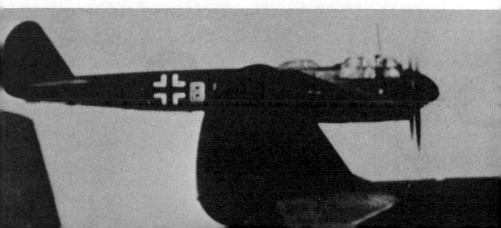

The new Fw 190 fighter, first introduced on the Channel Coast in mid-1941

the Ju 88 were still first class combat aircraft, but the same cannot be said for the Bf 110, the Ju 87 and the He 111, which had now reached the end of their development lives.

Not only was it in quality that the Germans were beginning to fall behind their enemies, but in quantity as well; with part of the vast industrial resources of the USA now being turned to the manufacture of combat aircraft, it was clear that unless German aircraft production was stepped up greatly the Luftwaffe was going to be swamped. Generalfeldmarschall Milch had made great strides to improve the supply of new aircraft since he had assumed responsibility for this, following Udet's suicide at the end of 1941, but there was still a long way to go. One of the steps he took to raise production was a programme to increase the work force by bringing to Germany skilled aircraft workers from the occupied countries. Special inducements, in the form of good pay and extra rations, were offered to encourage recruitment. These did attract the outsiders, but they were not sufficient to keep them once the heavy British air attacks began. This problem was aired during one of Milch's production conferences, when the following rather intriguing piece of dialogue took place between himself and Lucht and Kokotacky of the Messerschmitt company:

'Lucht: Recently a new problem has emerged. Of the Frenchmen whom we allow to go on leave, only half at most ever come back.

Milch: Of the eastern workers eighty per cent don't come back. I wouldn't let them go on leave at all.

Kokotacky: We have stopped all leave now.

Milch: You will have to give them something else to amuse themselves, so that they won't want to go . . .

Lucht: Once again, it is our top-class specialists that have stayed away.

Milch: I wouldn't have let the top-class specialists out of my hands anyway.

Lucht: But they are married, and that's what our orders are.

Milch: Well, they will find something else. You will have to set up a proper brothel there. That's what they are doing everywhere . . . He who works hardest gets a girl. You have only to put your heads together with the security services, and tell them "fix one for us". It doesn't matter if it costs something. That is not so bad.

Lahs: There is a special agency that is doing that, called "Homesteads Ltd" (*Heimstätten GmbH*). They are setting-up those things.

Milch: Lahs – would you like to see about this for us? I have the impression that you, with your worldly wiseness, know more of these things than

I do.

Lahs: I only want to say that Oberst Frey does that.

Milch: That is very intelligent. You can't let the people run round free in the German forests. You have to bring a bit of order into it all.'

Within the first months of 1943 there came the expected pointers that the year would see a marked hottening of the air war over Germany. On 27th January the American 8th Air Force opened a new phase in the Allied bomber offensive when fifty-five B-17s made a daylight attack on Wilhelmshaven. Three days later, much to Göring's chagrin, British Mosquito bombers attacked Berlin, also in broad daylight.

Between 27th January and the middle of July 1943, the 8th Air Force flew forty operational missions, of which twenty-seven were against U-boat bases and supply depots, and the remainder on industrial targets and airfields. For the most part these attacks were on targets in occupied Europe rather than in Germany, and their scale did remain modest – only at the end of the period did it become commonplace for more than one hundred heavy bombers to take part. Nevertheless it was clear to the Luftwaffe that the Americans were continually expanding their strategic bomber arm, and much heavier attacks on Germany could soon be expected.

Meanwhile, the effectiveness of the British night attacks had increased markedly, with the fitting of the 'Oboe' and 'H2S' precision blind bombing radar sets into the pathfinder aircraft. In a series of powerful raids Essen, Düsseldorf, Bochum, Dortmund, Krefeld, Wuppertal, Wilhelmshaven, Duisburg and Kiel all suffered serious damage.

To meet these new threats, the Germans expanded their air defences. Between the beginning of the year and the end of July 1943 the single-engined fighter force in the west increased from 635 aircraft to about 800. Over the same period the night fighter force increased from 414 aircraft to over 600. Since March the Luftwaffe had employed the night fighters in increasing numbers against the American day bombers. Although the night fighter crews – used as they

were to close-range engagements in the dark – invariably suffered heavier losses than their counterparts in the single-engined fighters, they did have the advantage that they were able to range far and wide over Germany after the bomber formations.

Initially the pilots of the lightly armed Messerschmitt 109Gs and Focke Wulf 190As had found it difficult to concentrate their fire for long enough to cause fatal damage to the tough B-17s and B-24s. Now the former had its armament increased from one 20mm and two 7.9mm machine guns to three 20mm cannon and two 13mm machine guns, the latter from two 20mm cannon and two 7.9mm machine guns to four 20mm cannon and two 13mm machine guns. During the summer of 1943 many of the German single- and twin-engined fighters were modified to carry respectively two or four under-wing launching tubes for the hefty 210mm Wgr 21 rockets, unguided missiles which could be fired from outside the range of the American bombers' defensive fire.

Simultaneously, the flak arm had also expanded greatly. The strength of the individual heavy batteries was increased from four to six and later eight guns; at the same time, increasing numbers of the newer and more powerful 105mm and 128mm guns came into operation to supplement the 88mm weapons.

So it was that the German air defences prepared themselves for the great battle; if it was to be a repeat of the Battle of Britain, with massed formations of bombers endeavouring to fight their way through the defences in daylight, then the Luftwaffe was ready. So far as the British night attacks were concerned, the defences were knocking down a good number – during the month of June 1943 they had shot down 275. The network of *Himmelbett* ground radar stations was still expanding, and this, coupled with the steady increase in the number of night fighters, gave rise to hopes that the Royal Air Force's losses would rise markedly during the months to follow.

Clearly, the climax of the air war over Germany could not be long delayed. But first, let us take a look at what had happened in the south.

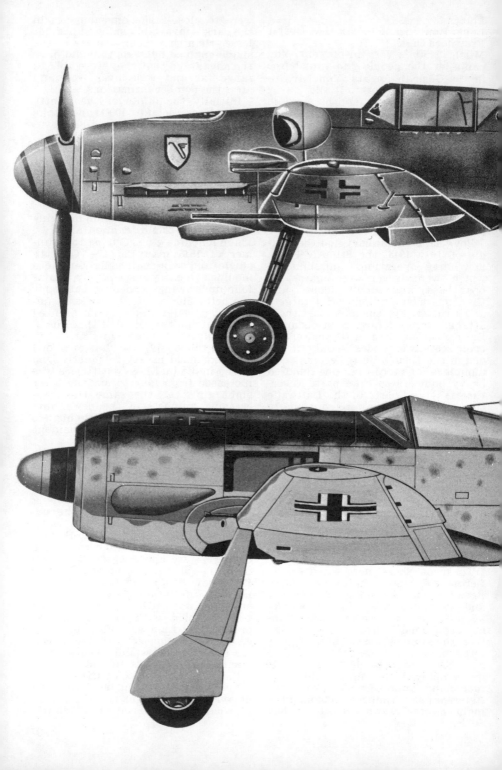

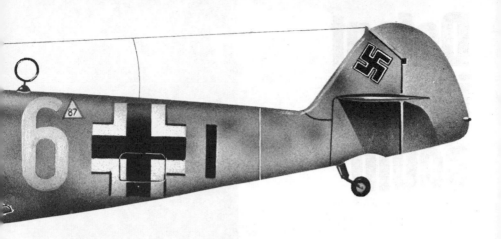

Messerschmitt Bf 109G-10
Engine: Daimler Benz DB 605D, developing 2,000 hp
for take off. *Armament:* One 30mm cannon and two 13mm machine guns.
Maximum speed: 428 mph at 24,000 feet. *Climb rate:* Six minutes to 20,000 feet.
Ceiling: 40,000 feet. *Range:* 350 miles. *Span:* 32 feet 6½ inches.
Length: 29 feet 8 inches

Focke Wulf 190A-5
Engine: BMW 801D-2 hp 17,000. *Armament:* Two 20mm cannon, two 7.9mm
machine guns. *Maximum speed:* 408 mph at 20,600 feet. *Climb:* 2,350 feet per
minute. *Ceiling:* 37,400 feet. *Range:* 500 miles. *Weights:* Empty 7,000 lbs; loaded
10,800 lbs. *Span:* 34 feet 5½ inches. *Length:* 29 feet

Defeat in the south

While the Luftwaffe made ready to defend the German homeland against the incursions of the Allied bombers, things had altered considerably for it in the south.

As we have seen, the Germans had lifted their pressure on Malta in the late spring of 1941, at the time of the preparations for the attack on Russia. During this lull the island was able to build up its potential as a base for destroyers, submarines and aircraft attacking the Axis sea supply routes to North Africa. By the autumn the losses inflicted were assuming serious proportions: in September nearly forty per cent of the German and Italian supplies dispatched across the Mediterranean were lost en route; during the following month the figure exceeded sixty per cent and in November nearly eighty per cent of the supplies failed to arrive; a major part of these losses were caused by Malta-based air and naval units.

Clearly something would have to be done about Britain's island bastion in the Mediterranean. In spite of the needs of the Russian front at the end of 1941, the Germans pulled back some 200 combat aircraft and moved them to bases in Sicily, for the attack on Malta. The force continued to expand, and by March 1942 more than 400 aircraft were available. This powerful attacking force quickly made its presence felt over Malta. Things reached a climax during April and May, when a total of 11,000 sorties were flown over the island. The British air and naval bases suffered heavily, and most of the surviving destroyers and anti-shipping aircraft had to be withdrawn.

Meanwhile, all attempts to push supplies through to the beleaguered island were met by the full force of the Luftwaffe. In March 1942 the Royal Navy was forced to employ an anti-aircraft ship, four cruisers and eighteen destroyers to escort a convoy of four merchantmen to Malta. In spite of this powerful covering screen, the Luftwaffe sank one of the ships, forced another to run aground, damaged, on Malta itself, with the result that only a small proportion of its fuel cargo could be unloaded, and hit the remaining two while they were in the process of discharging in Valetta harbour; only one fifth of the 26,000 tons of sorely-needed supplies dispatched was safely landed.

Meanwhile, in North Africa the Luftwaffe had by the spring of 1942 built up to a force of 260 aircraft, in addition to the Italian contingent, 340 strong. Combined, this force was more than twice as strong as that of the Royal Air Force in the area, and moreover, the newly-received Bf 109F fighters were superior to the Hurricanes and P-40 Tomahawks opposing them. On 26th May General Erwin Rommel's *Afrika Korps* went on to the offensive. With strong air support it thrust south, then eastwards round the British defensive line at Gazala. The southermost point of the line, at Bir Hakeim, now became the centre of gravity of the battle. By making a total of 1,400 sorties against this position, which was held with great stubbornness by men of the Free French Brigade, the Luftwaffe made a sizable contribution to its fall on 11th June. Once he was past the Gazala line Rommel kept going, and by again bringing heavy air support to bear the Germans were able to storm and capture the British fortress at Tobruk on 20th June. But for the rest of the German advance, which continued on deep into Egypt and was stopped only at El Alamein, the Luftwaffe was a spent force; during the intensive flying it had used up the fuel stocks so carefully accumulated during the previous months.

With the British forces defending Malta now at their weakest, and further away than ever from help from outside, the Germans and Italians gave very serious consideration to the idea of an airborne invasion of the island: Operation 'Hercules'. However, the fear of a repetition of what had happened in Crete – when the German airborne units had suffered very heavy losses – coupled with the success of Rommel's summer offensive which promised to make such an operation superfluous, finally decided Hitler against ordering the operation.

At the end of May 1942 the situation seemed to be well in hand for the Germans, and the greater part of the long range bomber force was moved from Sicily back to Russia to support the summer offensive there. But in spite of this the Luftwaffe was still strong enough to react vigorously to any attempt to resupply Malta. The next effort, in June, involved two separate convoys to the island: one from Egypt in the east, and one from Gibraltar in the west. The eastern convoy was turned back by the Italian navy, while the western one – comprising six merchant ships escorted by a battleship, two aircraft carriers, an anti-aircraft ship, three cruisers and seventeen destroyers, was severely mauled by German and Italian aircraft; only two of the six merchantmen reached Malta.

In August 1942 yet another convoy set out for the island, this time with fourteen merchant ships escorted by three aircraft carriers, two battleships, an anti-aircraft ship, six cruisers and twenty-four destroyers. At this time the Germans had some 220 aircraft based in Sicily; in addition the Italians had 300 there, and a further 130 on Sardinia.

The convoy was first sighted on the afternoon of 10th August, and for the action which followed the Germans reinforced the already strong anti-shipping force by some forty bombers. The next day the British force suffered a serious loss, when the aircraft carrier HMS *Eagle* was torpedoed and sunk by a U-boat which penetrated the destroyer screen. However, an attack by some thirty aircraft that evening was beaten off before it could do any damage, as was one of twenty more on the following morning. At mid-day on the 12th the Germans and Italians returned again, this time in much greater force, with an attack by some seventy fighters and torpedo and dive bombers. The aircraft carrier HMS *Victorious* suffered a very close shave: she was hit by a heavy bomb, but the weapon broke up on her armoured flight deck and caused little damage. The only other loss was of one of the merchantmen which was seriously damaged, forced to leave the convoy, and was later sunk. At 1830 hours that evening the attackers were back again in strength, this time with nearly a hundred aircraft. During this action the aircraft carrier HMS *Indomitable*

The German fighter ace Hans-Joachim Marseille, credited with 158 victories over British and US aircraft

– one of the primary targets – was hit three times with heavy bombs and had her flight deck put out of action. Now there was only one aircraft carrier left which was able to continue operating aircraft. A further air attack at last light on the 12th, by twenty aircraft, sank two merchant ships and damaged a third.

During the early morning darkness of the 13th, Italian motor torpedo boats made two highly successful attacks, which resulted in damage to a cruiser, the loss of four merchant ships and damage to a fifth. When dawn broke on the 13th the convoy was within range of RAF fighters based on Malta, but in spite of this three more air attacks were launched against it, the largest with twenty bombers. These resulted in the sinking of three merchant ships and damage to a fourth.

Thus it was that only five out of the fourteen merchantmen which originally set out reached Malta, and two of these were seriously damaged. But the 32,000 tons of cargo brought by these five was to provide sufficient sustenance for the island to keep going until the situation in North Africa had improved markedly in the Allies' favour.

While the British strove valiantly to keep Malta provisioned, the Ger-

German guided missiles. *Top:* The Henschel 293 rocket powered glider bomb carried a 1,100 pound warhead and was radio guided to its target by an operator using a small joy-stick controller. *Above:* The Fritz X guided bomb weighed 3,300 pounds, and was controlled in the same way as the Hs 293. *Left:* Major Bernhard Jope, who led the famous attack with Fritz X missiles on the Italian battle fleet mans and Italians had their own supply problems. With more and more British and American long range bombers becoming available in Egypt, the losses to Axis ships in the Mediterranean once more became serious. Moreover, the concentrated bombing attacks on the entry ports at Benghazi and Tobruk caused still further losses. During the summer of 1942 the Allied blockade of North Africa became almost total, and in desperation the Germans had to resort to airlifting in supplies of fuel. Thus the fighting power of the Luftwaffe in the area rapidly fell away, at a time when the Royal Air Force in Egypt was receiving large-scale reinforcements.

When the British launched their own offensive, at El Alamein on 23rd October 1942, the Royal Air Force was supreme. The Luftwaffe was to be seen only as a trail of wrecked aircraft left behind on airfields which had had to be abandoned as the *Afrika Korps* retreated further and further westwards. Rommel pulled his forces back in masterly fashion,. and the great retreat never did become a rout. But by the time it ended, at the beginning of 1943, the German and Italian forces had been driven out of both Egypt and Libya, and were fighting hard to retain a foothold in Tunisia.

The very speed of the British advance out of Egypt, coupled as it was with the simultaneous Anglo-American landings in Algeria and Morocco in the west, placed the Germans in a very difficult position; unless something was done quickly, they and the Italians would be thrown into the sea. Now, when almost all had been lost, Hitler decreed that the long-requested reinforcements should be sent to the Mediterranean theatre – this in spite of the vital necessity of moving combat units to Russia to stabilise the front there following the encirclement of the *Sixth Army* at Stalingrad. Accordingly the Luftwaffe units in North Africa, now formed into a single operational command, *Fliegerkorps Tunis*, suddenly came to life again; notable amongst the reinforcements were two units equipped with the Focke Wulf 190 fighter and which had been moved in from the Channel coast area. As

a result the Germans were able to gain a temporary air superiority over the British and American air forces in North Africa; quite apart from their advantage in having the most up-to-date fighters available, the Luftwaffe was operating from well-prepared bases and had only short lines of communications, while its opponents were forced to use makeshift airstrips and had very tenuous supply lines.

On 14th February 1943 Rommel launched his own offensive in Tunisia, Operation *'Frühlingswind'* (Spring Breeze). His targets were the newly-committed American units in the area of the Kasserine Pass, and for the occasion *Fliegerkorps Tunis* was able to assemble a force of 371 combat aircraft. At first all went well for the Germans, but after a week of heavy fighting their thrusts were contained by the British, French and American forces. A second German offensive at the end of February, this time against General Montgomery's seasoned 8th Army in the east, was thrown back with heavy losses.

But for all their efforts, the Germans could now do no more than delay the inevitable. While Allied ground forces gradually squeezed the pocket in Tunisia smaller, their air forces – whose equipment now included the latest versions of the Spitfire – were receiving adequate supplies and were rapidly gaining in effectiveness. In the mean time the position of *Fliegerkorps Tunis* got steadily worse and worse, as the American and British sea and air blockading forces set about the systematic strangulation of the Axis supply lines. By the middle of April 1943 the Luftwaffe in North Africa was on the verge of a complete breakdown; its few remaining airfields were being pounded regularly by Allied bombers, while American and British fighters often mounted standing patrols overhead. In the face of sustained pressure from Allied ground forces the final German defensive line cracked, then broke wide open. With nowhere left to retreat to the German and Italian troops began to surrender in large numbers, and by 13th May 1943 the whole of the African continent had finally been cleared. Nearly 250,000 Axis troops laid down their arms in Tunisia, in a disaster exceeded at this date only by that suffered by the Germans at Stalingrad.

On 3rd July 1943 the strength of the Luftwaffe in the Mediterranean totalled 1,280 aircraft.

This was when the Allied air forces began attacking the airfields in Sicily, in preparation for the seaborne assault on the island. When the first British and American troops waded ashore, one week later, the number of combat aircraft available to the Luftwaffe was reduced by more than a hundred. Because their airfields on Sicily had been bombed to the point of uselessness, the surviving Fw 190 ground attack aircraft had all to be withdrawn to bases in the Naples area, where they were in no position to contest the Allied landings. Meanwhile, the strength of the Allied fighter cover was such that the German level bomber force was able to achieve little, and *Gruppen* were cut to pieces whenever they tried.

On 17th August 1943 the last of the German troops remaining in Sicily surrendered, and now the Western Allies prepared for the invasion of the mainland of Italy. The Luftwaffe had suffered serious losses during the previous month, but because of the demands of the home and the Russian fronts these could not all be made good. Thus when the British and American troops landed on the toe of Italy, on 3rd September, the German strength in the Mediterranean theatre had fallen to a total of some 800 aircraft of all types. The Luftwaffe commander in Italy, Generalfeldmarschall von Richthofen, prudently decided to preserve his shrinking force for the more decisive battles that would certainly follow, and as a result the initial German reaction to the landings was weak.

On 10th September the Italians, now thoroughly sick and tired of the war, announced their capitulation, actually signed on 5rd September. That morning, under the terms of the armistice which had been negotiated during the previous weeks, the Italian battle fleet left its base at La Spezia for Malta, in order to surrender. But, unknown to the Italians, the Germans had learnt about the plan to surrender the fleet and had prepared accordingly. At Istres in the south of France the Do 217s of *III/KG 100* had been standing by for just such a move by the Italian warships, and now its commander, Major Bernhard Jope, led his bombers into action. Under its starboard wing, tucked between the engine and the fuselage, each of the nine Dorniers carried a single 'Fritz X' bomb. This highly-secret weapon comprised a 3,300 pound winged bomb, with a radio control mechanism built into the tail to enable the missile to be controlled from the releasing aircraft during the final part of its trajectory. Jope's Dorniers caught up with the Italian fleet just as the latter was in the narrow straits which seperate Corsica and Sardinia, and each aircraft ran in to bomb. Far below the attackers, the Italian ships went into tight turns in an effort to put the Germans off their aim. In the face of normal high-level bombing such tactics would have been successful: a bomb takes nearly three quarters of a minute to fall from 20,000 feet, during which time a fast ship in open water can cover 700 yards. But Jope's aircraft were attacking with radio-controlled bombs, and these manoeuvres afforded the ships little protection. After releasing the missile, the bomb aimer in the nose of each Dornier concentrated his attention on the tracking flare in the rear of each bomb; he carefully 'steered' the flare until it appeared right over the ship selected as target, then applied corrections to hold it there.

The first hit was on the Italian flagship, the battleship *Roma*. The Fritz X impacted on the starboard side of the rear mast, punched its way clean through the ship, and exploded as it was emerging underneath it. Her starboard turbines wrecked, the ship's speed fell to sixteen knots. A few minutes later a second missile hit *Roma*, this time between the bridge and her 'B' turret. The bomb smashed the turbines on the port side, and the battleship wallowed to a halt. Meanwhile, below decks, a fierce fire was raging unchecked and the ship's crew signalled that she was in 'a desperate condition'. Finally, the flames reached the forward magazine and ignited the ammunition stored there. In the tremendous explosion which followed *Roma* folded up like a jack-knife, then broke into two and sank. Most of her crew went down with her.

Soon after the attack on *Roma* her sister-ship, the *Italia*, was hit on the bows by a Fritz X; she shipped some 900 tons of water, but was able to make her way to Malta under her own steam.

Jope and his men were denied the satisfaction of seeing the *Roma* go down. Recently he recalled : 'We did not see the *Roma* explode. That happened after we left. We saw the explosions as the bombs hit, sure, but how often had we seen this before and then the ship managed to limp back to port?' Only later, when the news was given out in an Allied news broadcast, did the men of *III/KG 100* learn how successful their attack with the new guided weapons had been.

On the same day as the Italian fleet set sail, Allied troops stormed ashore at Salerno near Naples. This was the time for action for which Richthofen had been husbanding his force, and he hurled his units against the bridgehead. Moreover, the concentration of shipping offshore was just the sort of target for which the Fritz X had been designed, and Jope's men pressed home their attacks; in the week that followed they .scored hits on the battleship HMS *Warspite*, and the cruisers HMS *Uganda* and USS *Savanna*, causing serious damage to all three.

The reader may gain some idea of the destructive power of the Fritz X from the damage *Warspite* suffered when a salvo of three of these missiles hit her. One bomb scored a direct hit which penetrated six decks to explode on, and blow a hole through, the double bottom; the other two bombs gashed her side compartments. One boiler room was demolished, and four of her other five were flooded. Luckily for the British sailors there was no fire, or the results might have been as disastrous as they had been in the case of *Roma*. As it was the ship could not be steered, she could not raise steam, and for want of power her guns were out of action. The battleship took on 5,000 tons of water. In view of the magnitude of the damage, it is little short of miraculous that the casualties on board were limited to nine killed and fourteen wounded. *Warspite* had to be towed back to Malta for temporary repairs, and she was not fit for action again until June 1944.

III/KG 100 kept up its effort against the shipping, in conjunction with other units launching another guided weapon, the Henschel 293 glider bomb; however, during the Salerno battle the latter weapon achieved little. Then fighter cover for the Allies became available over the bridgehead from bases ashore, and the German bomber units began to lose heavily. Meanwhile German fighter-bombers, including Bf 109s equipped with 21cm rocket launchers which they used against targets on the ground, kept up a steady pressure on the troops ashore. The Luftwaffe fought a spirited action until 20th September; then, British troops advancing up from the south threatened the German bases in the Foggia area, and the fighter-bomber units had to pull back.

So it was that the Luftwaffe found itself overwhelmed over the Mediterranean, able to cause disconcerting but by no means decisive damage to the American and British invasion fleets. The Fritz X and Hs 293 guided weapons, on which the Germans had placed such great hopes, seemed at first to be the answer to the problem of smashing attempted seaborne landings; but once there was adequate fighter cover over the bridgehead it was the German launching aircraft which suffered the heavy losses.

Now the Western Allies were at last firmly established on the mainland of Europe. But because of its mountainous spine, Italy is a difficult country to advance up and the German commander there, Kesselring, found little difficulty in delaying the invaders. In the meantime, one of the greatest battles of the war was being fought out deep in Russia, for Hitler had decided to smash the Red Army once and for all in one giant set-piece battle.

Russia: a force bled white

Shot-down Junkers 88 on display in
Sverdlov Square, Moscow

The loss of North Africa had been a serious setback to the Axis cause, but it was obvious to both sides that the really decisive battle of 1943 would be fought in Russia. Hitler was determined to regain the initiative in the east, which had been lost so disastrously at Stalingrad; he decided to do this with a massive set-piece double pincer movement, to wipe out the troublesome Russian salient round Kursk in the central part of the front. The offensive was to be code-named 'Zitadelle' (Citadel), and on 15th April 1944 Hitler had said of it: 'This attack is of decisive importance. It must succeed quickly and completely. It must put the initiative for this spring and summer in our hands. All preparations must therefore be made with the greatest care and energy; the best units, the best weapons, the best commanders, and large quantities of ammunition shall be committed in the areas of the main effort. Every commander and every man must be filled with the decisive meaning of this attack. The victory at Kursk must have the effect of a beacon for the entire world.'

Along a front of only 120 miles, the German army concentrated 900,000 men with 10,000 guns and 2,700 tanks. For its part the Luftwaffe assembled 1,800 combat aircraft to provide air support for the twin thrusts. The southern arm of the pincer was to be covered by Luftflotte IV, under General Otto Dessloch, with 1,100 aircraft; the northern arm by Fliegesdivision 1, under Generalmajor Paul Deichmann, with the remaining 700 machines. Overhead, reconnaissance aircraft of the Luftwaffe photographed every square yard of the defences; as the German General Mellenthin later wrote: 'No offensive was ever prepared as carefully as this one.' The Germans were confident of success: it was summer, and the Russians would have no Generals 'Mud' and 'Winter' to turn to for help this time. However, the massive German build-up was not missed by the vigilant Russian Intelligence service, and the Red Army massed even greater forces of its own within and behind the salient.

The German army opened its attacks towards Kursk on the morning of 5th July, and right from the start the Luftwaffe ground-attack and bomber units operated intensively over the battlefield to support the advancing armoured formations. The newly committed Henschel 129B tank-busting aircraft, commanded by Hauptmann Bruno Meyer, proved to be an outstanding success against the Russian tanks. On 9th July this unit came upon a Russian brigade, supported by some forty tanks, moving up towards the flank of the southernmost German thrust. Wave after wave of the specialised and heavily armoured ground-attack machines swept in to attack the troops on the ground. When they attacked the tanks the German pilots aimed their tungsten-cored 30mm cannon shells at the sides and rear parts, where the armour was at its thinnest, and knocked out several tanks. The air-ground battle lasted about an hour, after which the badly mauled Russian force pulled back in some disorder.

But in spite of the usual powerful support from the Luftwaffe, the German armoured thrusts on the ground were able to advance only with the greatest difficulty. Fighting stubbornly from well-prepared 'hedgehog' positions, the Russians made them pay heavily for every yard. Moreover, the Red Air Force, present in enormous strength over the battlefield, often got through the German fighter screen and mounted air strikes on the advancing units and their supporting elements.

With the two claws of the German pincer firmly embedded in the defensive positions to the north and the south of Kursk, the Russian High Command judged the time ripe to launch the counteroffensive. At the centre of the front the line was in the shape of a reversed letter 'S', with the German salient in the north at Orel pointing eastwards, and the Russian salient in the south at Kursk pointing westwards. On 12th July the Russian armour punched its way through the defences round the Orel salient, and began to advance rapidly westward. The German troops moving on Kursk from the north were immediately placed on the defensive, and reserves which had been ear-

The changing German front in Russia

Above: Bf 109 fighter camouflaged at the side of its airfield in Russia, 1943.
Below: Ju 87 operating in the tank-busting role, fitted with two
37mm Flak 18 cannon; such aircraft were used a great deal over Russia

marked for the main German thrust now had to be rushed to the threatened sector. *Luftflotte VI*, whose units included *Fliegerdivision 1*, went into action round Orel to try to stop or at least slow the Russian assault, to buy time for the German troops trying to re-establish the line. Initially the Russians' move was through wooded countryside, and by the skilful use of camouflage they were able to avoid the attentions of the Luftwaffe. But then the armoured force emerged into open country. With still only weak forces on the ground to oppose the move, the Germans had to stake everything on the effectiveness of the ground-attack and anti-tank aircraft of the Luftwaffe. The forces concentrated, and within a short time virtually every German battle-worthy fighting *Gruppe* in Russia was engaged over the Orel salient; flying several sorties on each day, the aircraft bombed and strafed the advancing Russians on 19th, 20th and 21st July. By such desperate measures, the German army was given sufficient time to reform its defensive line.

The intensity of the air operations was even greater than the German planners had allowed for, and in the closing stages of the Kursk battle the Luftwaffe suffered from its perennial shortage of fuel. For its part the Red Air Force had no such hinderance, and the Germans were nowhere able to establish any real air superiority. By maintaining pressure from the air and the ground on the Orel salient the Russians slowly squeezed the Germans out of it, while other attacks on the flanks of the thrusts towards Kursk forced the Germans back to their jumping-off positions. On 23rd July Hitler called off the offensive. The battle of Kursk, on which so much had been staked, was lost to the Germans; it was to be their last full scale offensive in the east.

For the rest of 1943 the actions in the east were characterised by the same factors which had proved decisive during the final phases of the actions at Kursk and Orel: German numerical inferiority and Russian numerical and supply superiority and strategic initiative. And all the time the events on other fronts were to aggravate matters. As we have seen, during 1943 the Mediterranean front had become a veritable mincing-machine for Luftwaffe combat units, but because of the need to bolster the Italians these had been replenished – usually at the expense of the Eastern Front – although not to full strength. On top of this, the steady increase in the demands of the home defences had resulted in still further withdrawals of fighters from the east; in September 1943 six *Geschwader* of fighters were pulled back for this purpose.

Following the repulse of the German summer offensive, the Luftwaffe concentrated the main part of its strength in support of the army units struggling to hold the line of the Donets river. But the air force was overextended, and the Germans were forced to adopt a makeshift policy of switching units from one end of the line to the other in response to the varying Russian pressures.

The Russians were quick to exploit the German weaknesses. In a series of well co-ordinated thrusts they squeezed the Germans out of Kharkov and Taganrog in the south. Then, while the Germans were still under extreme pressure in that area, they went on to the offensive in the centre of the front where Luftwaffe strength had fallen to only 500 aircraft, covering a line extending nearly 400 miles – and many of these were not combat machines but army co-operation and reconnaissance types. As a result the new thrust was backed by almost total Russian air superiority, and the important cities of Bryansk and Smolensk fell to the advancing troops on 17th and 25th September respectively.

When the Germans shifted aircraft and reinforcements to the centre, the Russians resumed their advance in the south, and at the beginning of

October, they stormed their way through the planned German last stand 'Eastern Rampart' line on the Dniepr River. Only by concentrating all available bombers and ground attack aircraft back in the south, and by flying these on several sorties per day for a period of five days, was the Luftwaffe able to slow the advance sufficiently for the German army to halt it just short of Krivoy Rog.

But, as usual, such concentration was possible only at the expense of the other sectors, and now the Russians skilfully struck once again in the centre. On 6th November they took Kiev, and then advanced on Zhitomir. The resultant critical situation called for the most desperate measures on the part of the Germans, who were forced yet again to collect, move, and concentrate their now almost exhausted air and ground forces 200 miles to the north of the previous centre of operations near Krivoy Rog. In this they were successful, and the Russians were held.

When the weather broke, and the autumn mud season put an end to mobile operations on the ground, the Germans found themselves holding a precarious line which was in some places almost 400 miles back from where it had been at the beginning of 1944. In the extreme south, the Crimean peninsula, now cut off, had to be kept supplied in the face of Russian interference, and this imposed a steady drain on German air and sea transport resources. And despite the continued Russian pressure on the central part of the front the Luftwaffe in the east now had to hold nearly two thirds of its combat strength (1,150 out of 1,750 aircraft) in the south because of the need to hold the Russians clear of the Rumanian oilfields which were so vital to the German war economy.

At the close of 1944 the Luftwaffe in the east was no longer powerful enough to have any decisive influence on the situation on the ground. Outnumbered by two or even three to one by the steadily improving Russian air forces – whose aircraft were in many cases now as good as their German counterparts – the German *Gruppen* could at best only delay by a little the steamroller Russian thrusts, and this usually at a heavy cost in both men and machines. From now on there would be little extra to spare for the Eastern Front, for soon the Luftwaffe would have to fight for its very life over Germany itself.

By the end of 1944, the Luftwaffe was losing heavily in the East

In defence of the homeland

The summer of 1943 had seen a steady movement of day fighter units back to Germany, ready to ward off the expected American deep penetration daylight bombing attacks. Simultaneously, the Luftwaffe night fighters force had also been expanding, to meet the increasingly powerful attacks on German cities at night by the British.

It was to be the Royal Air Force which struck the first blow against the Luftwaffe in the newly intensified battle over Germany.

As we have seen, the ground radar-controlled night fighters had been knocking down bombers at a rate too great for the comfort of the British. It was clear that if the night attacks were to continue, some means would have to be devised to neutralise the devastatingly efficient German system. Technically, the answer was very simple: little strips of aluminium foil. Know by the cover-name 'Window', the strips each measured twelve inches long by one-and-a-half inches wide, and came in bundles of 2,000 held together by an elastic band. When released from an aircraft the bundle broke up, to form a 'cloud' of radar-reflective strips which gave a 'blip' on the radar screens the same size as that from a four-engined bomber. By releasing one such bundle per minute from each aircraft in a concentrated bomber stream, it was possible to saturate the area with 'blips', and thus make radar-controlled fighter interceptions impossible.

During 1942 scientists in both Britain and Germany had carried out tests with the metal strips, quite independently and under the greatest secrecy. In both countries the men had reached exactly the same conclusion: the new counter to radar was dynamite. If it was used properly, then it could wreck the radar-dependent night air defences of either country. At that time neither side had felt that it had a sufficiently great margin of strength over its opponent to justify the risk of retaliation in kind. But by the summer of 1943 the striking power of Royal Air Force Bomber Command had expanded out of all recognition, while the demands of the war of attrition on the Eastern Front had reduced the German strategic bomber force to comparative impotence. On 15th July 1943, during a meeting of the British War Cabinet, Mr Churchill gave his permission for 'Window' to be used against the Germans.

So it came about that ten days later, during the 791 bomber raid on Hamburg on the night of 24th July, the new countermeasure was used in action. The effect was devastating: it reduced the German defences to chaos, utter and complete. As usual the night fighters orbited over their radio beacons, awaiting instructions from their controllers on the ground. But none came. Instead the ether was thick with confused appeals and exclamations:

'The enemy are reproducing themselves!'

'It is impossible – too many hostiles.'

'Wait a while. There are many more hostiles.'

'I cannot control you. Try without your ground control.'

When the night fighter crews tried to seek out targets using their own radar sets, they soon found themselves making attacks on the swirling clouds of 'Window'.

When the first wave of bombers arrived over Hamburg their crews were struck by the air of unreality at the target: instead of the usual precise handling of the searchlights, they now all seemed to be groping blindly. Where the beams did cross others would quickly join them, and as many as thirty or forty beams would build up to form a monster cone – on nothing at all.

The radar sets which controlled the searchlights were now useless, and so were those which directed the guns. The gunners were forced to abandon predicted fire, and instead the men loosed off round after unaimed round ineffectively into the black sky above.

That night the Royal Air Force lost only twelve aircraft, one and a half per cent of the large attacking force. Clearly the 'Window' countermeasure had been an outstanding success; had the raid cost the normal six per cent loss rate during the previous attacks on Hamburg, the force

Allied targets in Germany

would have been depleted by about fifty aircraft. So about thirty-five bombers and more than 200 trained crewmen had been saved, by the dropping of forty tons of 'Window' – ninety-two million strips of aluminium foil.

The first attack on Hamburg had been bad enough for the Germans, but worse was to follow: three nights later the British returned to the city, this time with 722 bombers. With the city's water supplies disrupted and the civil defence headquarters smashed in the previous raid, the torrent of well-placed incendiary bombs caused fires which were soon raging unchecked. The smaller fires linked together and, as the heated air rose up, more air rushed in to take its place. This fanned the flames, before itself becoming heated and rising. The process repeated itself over and over again, while all the time the flames blazed hotter. The result was a fire storm. Soon, in places, the temperature exceeded 1,000° Centigrade, and the mighty convection currents produced winds of up to 150 miles per hour – nearly twice hurricane force. Within a short time, a built-up area 3½ miles long and 2½ miles wide was burning itself to death: nine square miles of fire. In the air raid shelters underneath the city people were trapped, and the bunkers where they had sought safety became their crematoria.

Meanwhile, overhead, the Luftwaffe was as impotent as it had been on the first occasion when the 'Window' had been used. The raiders lost only seventeen of their number – still a remarkably low figure considering the number of people engaged in the defence of the city.

On the morning of 29th July *Gauleiter* Kaufmann appealed to all non-essential civilians to leave Hamburg. They needed no second bidding. Between dawn and dusk nearly a million people, many of them swathed in bandages or hobbling on improvised crutches, streamed out of the stricken city.

On the morning of 30th July the British bombers returned yet again to what was now a ghost town, to carve out yet new swathes of destruction. At a conference held in Berlin that afternoon Generalfeldmarshall Milch declared: 'The attacks on Hamburg have affected the morale of the people. Unless we evolve a means of defeating these terror raids soon, an extremely difficult situation will arise.' But the hour had produced the man. It will be remembered that we last met Hauptmann Hajo Herrmann when he collided with the barrage balloon over Plymouth in June 1940. By the summer of 1944, Herrmann, now a famous bomber ace with the rank of major, was a lecturer in tactics at the Luftwaffe staff college near Berlin; and this imaginative airman was forever coming up with new and wild proposals. He had, for example, suggested a method of carrying the war to the American cities by means of a few large flying boats which could take on their fuel and bombs from U-boats; if half-a-dozen widely spaced U-boats were used, Herrmann had calculated from meteorological data that it would be possible for the flying boats to find calm enough water to alight, and so it would be possible to maintain the attack for sufficiently long to force the Americans to hold back large numbers of fighters for defence. Another of Herrmann's schemes was the capture of an Allied aircraft carrier, by means of commando troops landed on the flight deck in gliders. Both these ideas came to nothing because by 1943 the Germans had no effort to spare for such adventures.

Earlier in the summer Herrmann had proposed a new method of night fighting, employing single-seat fighters. Called '*Wilde Sau*' (wild boar), the tactics called for the concentration of the fighters over the target itself. There the massed searchlights, the fires on the ground and the British pathfinders' marker flares would combine to light up the sky for miles around, and thus silhouette the bombers for the fighters which could attack visually. And, since Herrmann's scheme made no use of precision radar, the British 'Window' countermeasure could not effect it at all.

Herrmann had tried out his ideas on a small scale earlier in July, before the Hamburg disaster, and had ach-

Distribution of German fighter planes

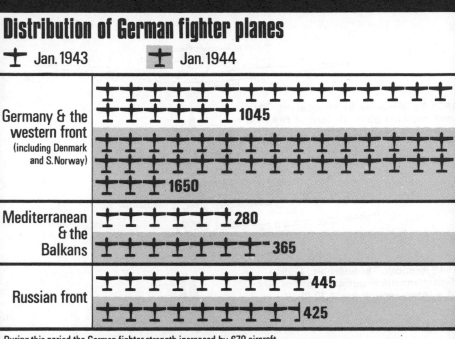

✈ Jan. 1943   ✈ Jan. 1944

Germany & the western front (including Denmark and S. Norway)	1045 (Jan. 1943) / 1650 (Jan. 1944)
Mediterranean & the Balkans	280 (Jan. 1943) / 365 (Jan. 1944)
Russian front	445 (Jan. 1943) / 425 (Jan. 1944)

During this period the German fighter strength increased by 670 aircraft; almost all of these were retained for home defence

1939 Supermarine Spitfire: eight ·303-inch machine guns. Weight of fire of a three-second burst 10 lb

1942 Republic Thunderbolt: eight 5-inch machine-guns. Weight of fire of a three-second burst 20 lb

1939 Messerschmitt Bf 109E: two 7.9-mm machine-guns and two 20-mm cannon. Weight of fire of a three-second burst 18 lb

1942 Hawker Typhoon: four 20-mm cannon. Weight of fire of a three-second burst 35 lb

1942 Messerschmitt Bf 109G: two 13-mm machine-guns and three 20-mm cannon. Weight of fire of a three-second burst 35 lb

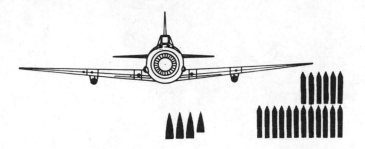

**1944 Focke Wulf Fw 190-A-4: two
7·9-mm machine-guns and four 20-mm
cannon. Weight of fire of a three-
second burst 37 lb; weight of two
Wgr 21 210-mm rockets which could
also be carried was 180 lb**

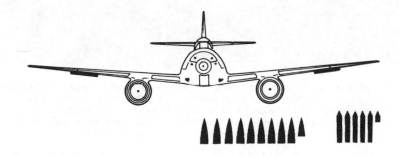

**1945 Messerschmitt Me 262: four
30-mm cannon. Weight of fire of a
three-second burst 96 lb; weight of
24 R4M 55-mm rockets which could
also be carried was 53 lb**

The figures above show each fighter's armament, with the weight of fire they
could deliver in a burst three seconds long. Of necessity the quoted figures are
approximate, for the rate of fire of weapons of the same type could vary by as
much as 10%

The vital importance of countering the heavily armoured American bombers
accelerated air-to-air weapon development in Germany, and at the end of the war
she had outstripped all other nations in this field

The use of rockets was an attempt to increase the weight of fire without
recourse to cumbersome heavy-calibre guns. In the case of the rockets, the
weight quoted is that of the warheads. The Wgr 21 was an improvised installation
using army rocket mortar bombs; the missiles were time fused to explode some
1,000 yards in front of the launching aircraft. Because of the difficulty of judging
this range accurately, the Wgr-21 scored few 'kills'. The smaller R4M rockets
were impact fused; they were aimed at a single aircraft target, and were fired in a
salvo. Potentially very effective against bomber formations, the R4M arrived in
service too late to have a significant effect upon events

Luftwaffe hoax. Propaganda photographs showing the Heinkel 100 fighter with fake unit markings and victory bars, although the type never saw service with a Luftwaffe unit and it is doubtful if it ever shot down anything. The type was billed as the 'He 113' and the ruse was successful: there are many reports of Allied pilots fighting battles with He 113s

ieved moderate success. Now that the *Himmelbett* tactics had been rendered ineffective, he received orders from Göring to bring into action as quickly as possible a full *Geschwader* of fighters for the 'Wild Boar' role. The new unit was *Jagdgeschwader 300*, and its Bf 109s and Fw 190s all carried underbelly fuel tanks to provide the extra range necessary for night operations. The 'Wild Boar' method was not a panacea – Herrmann had never claimed that it would be – but at least it would provide the German cities with some sort of defence while new radar equipment was produced which could work in the face of the 'Window' jamming.

The two-seater radar-equipped specialist night fighters could also engage in 'Wild Boar' operations over the target area. But to use their potential to the full, Oberst von Lossberg, another one-time bomber ace now employed in air defence, proposed the '*Zahme Sau*' (tame boar) method. His idea was for the now otherwise useless ground precision control stations to direct the two-seater fighters into the area where the 'Window' concentration was densest, and once there the German pilots were to seek out their targets visually. Lossberg hoped that eventually the night fighter crews would become familiar enough with the 'Tame Boar' tactics for it to be possible to set up long running battles which would last the whole time the raiders were over occupied Europe.

While the Luftwaffe High Command hastened to cobble together some sort of defence against the night attacks on Germany, things were coming to the boil by day as well.

By July 1943 the American 8th Air Force in Britain comprised fifteen heavy bomber groups with some 300 B-17s and B-24s. But for the daylight attackers there was no equivalent to 'Window' to blind the German fighters.

The Americans had stepped up their attacks on Germany in the summer of 1943 and matters came to a head on 17th August, when 146 B-17s with a fighter escort set out to attack the Messerschmitt assembly plant at Regensburg in southern Germany. It was to be the deepest penetration yet made into German airspace by the 8th Air Force. The defences were alerted early on of the approach of the formations by radar, but the German fighters waited patiently until lack of fuel forced the escorting Spitfires and Thunderbolts to turn for home. Then the Luftwaffe pounced. The defenders dived on the American formations from ahead and above, made a firing pass, then turned and came in for a second pass from the rear. Relays of fighter *Gruppen* repeated these tactics, and the subsequent running battle continued up to and past the target, for a distance of about 350 miles. As soon as they landed, the fighter units which had engaged first, those based in France, Holland and Belgium, were ordered to refuel and rearm ready to make further attacks on the bomber formations as they made their return flights to England. But the American planners had thought of that too, and the depleted formations continued southwards over the Mediterranean and landed at airfields in North Africa. In spite of this move, the force lost twenty-four of its number.

But the day had still to reach its climax. Even before the first wave of B-17s had attacked Regensburg a second force, this time of 229 bombers, was making for the vitally important ball-bearing factory complex at Schweinfurt. This time the German fighter pilots did not even wait for the American fighter escort to break away before they attacked. While some single-engined fighter *Gruppen* battled with the escorts, others swept in to rake the heavy bombers with cannon and machine gun fire. When the fighter escort had finally to withdraw yet more single- and twin-engined German fighters intercepted the attacking formations; many of them launched salvoes of 210mm rockets, each one with an explosive warhead weighing ninety pounds, into the bomber formations from outside the range of the defending .5-inch machine guns. Again the Luftwaffe fought a running battle along the route to the target, and, as the bombers were returning to their bases in England, during the homeward flight as well. Thirty-six bombers failed to return from the Schweinfurt attack.

The double attack on Regensburg and Schweinfurt cost the 8th Air Force sixty B-17s – sixteen per cent of the force which had taken off – and a further one hundred suffered varying degrees of damage. The Luftwaffe lost twenty-five fighters, and the pilots of most of these were able to bail out to safety.

Any jubilation felt in Germany over the Schweinfurt success was quickly dampened on that very evening, when a force of 498 bombers of the Royal Air Force smashed the German guided missile research establishment at Peenemünde. This, coming as it did on top of the disastrous setbacks suffered by the Luftwaffe first at Stalingrad, then in North Africa, Sicily, Kursk and Hamburg, was the final straw for the Chief of Staff Generaloberst Hans Jeschonnek. Jeschonnek had read the Intelligence reports on the vast American production plans for 1943, and he had seen the reconnaissance photographs of the airfields in Britain steadily being stocked with aircraft which proved the accuracy of the reports. A year earlier he had commented: 'If

we have not won the war by December 1942 we have no prospect of doing so.' The Germans had not won the war by December 1942. Now it was clear to him that the writing was on the wall for the Luftwaffe, that the force would be inexorably crushed by its enemies; the short war, on which he had staked everything, had not brought victory. On the morning of 18th August Jeschonnek shot himself. Just as in the case of Udet, nearly two years earlier, the circumstances behind the senior Luftwaffe commander's death were kept secret; it was announced that Jeschonnek had died of a 'haemorrhage of the stomach'. In his place as Chief of Staff of the Luftwaffe came General Günther Korten.

The reverse during the Regensburg and Schweinfurt attacks let to a change in American daylight bombing policy, and between then and 7th October only three out of the fifteen heavy bomber raids flown by the 8th Air Force were against targets in Germany – and none of these penetrated very far inland.

This lull lasted until 8th October

1943, and in the week that followed Bremen, Marienburg, Danzig and Münster were raided. The new series of attacks met the full force of the further strengthened German fighter force, and together cost the Americans eighty-three bombers.

The second climax in the American daylight bombing offensive came on 14th October, when a force of 291 B-17s set out to finish off the ball-bearing factories at Schweinfurt. This time the German fighter reaction was, in the words of the American official historians, 'unprecedented in its magnitude, in the cleverness with which it was planned, and in the severity with which it was executed'. Again there was a long running battle as wave after wave of ordinary cannon- and machine gun-armed fighters pressed home their attack on the bombers to close range, while others fired heavy calibre cannon and launched rockets from outside the range of the defensive fire. Any damaged bomber which fell away from the protection of its formation was immediately pounced on by the fighters and finished off.

Above: **Bf 109G.** *Left:* **Fw 190 carrying 210mm rockets. The two fighters which saw action in defence of the German homeland**

Many of the single-engined fighters were able to land and refuel and re-arm after their first attack, and go into action again as the bombers returned towards Britain after the attack. In all a total of about 300 single-engined fighters, forty twin-engined fighters, and a few night fighters went into action. As a result this second attack on Schweinfurt was a crippling disaster for the Americans. Sixty B-17s were shot down, seventeen had suffered severe damage, and 121 more returned with lesser damage. Thus out of the original force of 291 bombers which had set out from England in the morning, 199 were either destroyed or damaged. The B-17s defensive fire had caused the destruction of only thirty-eight German fighters, and damage to twenty more. Yet again the daylight bombing offensive against targets deep in Germany was stopped in its tracks.

For the Germans, the victory over the Schweinfurt attackers served to confirm the correctness of their defensive measures to counter the American daylight bomber raids: their large numbers of conventional single- and twin-engined fighters, fitted with medium and heavy calibre cannon and air-to-air rockets, could and did inflict unacceptably high losses on the bomber formations.

Since the summer of 1942 the revolutionary new Messerschmitt 262 jet fighter had been undergoing flight trials, and by mid-1943 the type was considered to be ready for series production. With a top speed in excess of 500 mph, the new aircraft was eagerly demanded by Generalmajor Adolf Galland for his fighter force. The machine was readied for service with the *Jagdgeschwader*.

But if at this time the Germans were well satisfied with the daylight defences of their homeland, their bomber force was still smarting after its failure to strike hard at the invading Allied troops once they had got ashore at Salerno during the invasion of Italy. It was against this background that Hitler watched a special demonstration of the Me 262 at Insterburg in East Prussia on 26th November 1943 – just over a month after the Schweinfurt victory. With test pilot Gerd Lintner at the controls the sixth prototype of the new jet performed impressively. Hitler casually asked Willi Messerschmitt, the machine's designer who was standing next to him, whether the Me 262 could carry any bombs. Just as casually, the latter replied that it could. To Hitler the sleek jet seemed to be the answer to his most pressing need for the Luftwaffe: a fast bomb-carrying aircraft which could penetrate even the powerful Allied fighter screens, and smash any Anglo-American attempt to get troops ashore on the coast of north-western Europe. So it was that Hitler's ideas began to crystalise. On 5th December Göring received the following telegram, signed by Hitler's Luftwaffe aide:

'The *Führer* has called our attention once more to the tremendous importance of the production of jet propelled aircraft for employment as fighter-bombers. It is imperative that the Luftwaffe have a number of jet fighter-bombers ready for front commitment by the spring of 1944. Any difficulties occasioned by labour and raw material shortages will be resolved by the exploitation of Luftwaffe resources, until such time as existing shortages can be made up.'

There can be little doubt that had many hundreds of the jet fighter-bombers been available, they would have proved a serious embarrassment to any Allied seaborne invasion attempt. But the decision to produce the Me 262 as a fighter-bomber meant that the machine had to be extensively modified and re-stressed to enable it to undertake its new role. And this all took time. The result was a delay in the type's introduction into service of about six months. And during these six months the most important air battle of the war, so far as the Germans were concerned, was to be lost to the Luftwaffe; it would be lost because the Luftwaffe lacked a really high performance fighter—like the Me 262. And in December 1943 there was no *vital* necessity for a very high performance fighter for home defence. So *at the time* that Hitler decided that the initial production batches of the Me 262 should be used in the fighter-bomber role, the decision was a reasonable one. It was reasonable as long as there was no

An Fw 190 under attack from an American fighter. A gun camera picture taken at the fatal moment

128

radical change in the air situation over Germany, and if the jet fighter-bomber could be made available in large numbers *in time* to go into action against any invasion attempt.

During the winter of 1943 the top-priority campaign by German scientists to produce equipment to counter the 'Window' tactics used by the British during their night raids, began to bear fruit. Now the first night fighters fitted with the new radar set, *SN-2*, became available in useful numbers of operations; because the *SN-2* worked on a much lower frequency than the earlier *Lichtenstein* set it replaced, it was not so badly affected by the 'Window' clouds. The introduction of the new radar, combined with the increased proficiency in the 'Tame Boar' tactics, was to have an important effect on the night battles during the winter of 1943-44.

On 3rd November 1943 Air Chief Marshal Sir Arthur Harris, the British bomber commander, had sent the following minute to Mr Churchill: 'We can wreck Berlin from end to end if the USAAF will come in on it. It may cost us 400-500 aircraft. It will cost Germany the war.' This was the sort of promise the Winston Churchill could not resist, and Harris received permission to launch what later became known as 'The Battle of Berlin'. But the USAAF, still licking its wounds after the disastrous attack on Schweinfurt, would not 'come in on it'. Harris decided to go it alone.

The first attack on Berlin in the new series was on the night of 18th November, and only nine out of the 444 aircraft engaged failed to return. There were three more attacks on the German capital in November and four in December; on each occasion bad weather prevented the defenders from inflicting serious losses, but, for the same reason, the bombing failed to achieve any degree of concentration.

Then, as the new year opened, the British losses began to rise alarmingly. The first of the great and costly battles was on 21st January, when 649 bombers struck at Magdeburg. Fifty-five failed to return. The bomber crews fought back hard, but succeeded in destroying only seven German night fighters. One of these was a Ju 88 flown by the then top-scoring night ace, Major Prince Heinrich zu Sayn-Wittgenstein. Wittgenstein was the commander of *NJG/2*, and had taken off from Stendal near Berlin at 2100 hours that evening on a 'Tame Boar' patrol. Now his radar operator, Feldwebel Ostheimer, takes up the story:

'At about 2200 hours I picked up the first contact on my [*SN-2*] radar. I gave the pilot directions and a little later our target was seen: it was a Lancaster. We moved into position and opened fire, and the aircraft immediately caught fire in the left wing. It went down at a steep angle and started to spin. Between 2200 and 2205 hours the bomber crashed and went off with a violent explosion. I

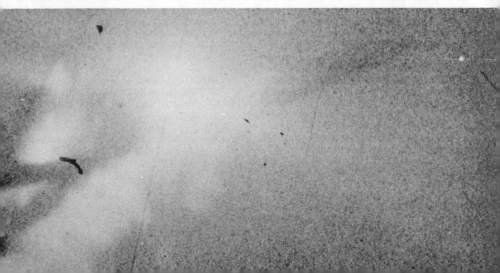

watched the crash.

'Again we searched. At times I could see as many as six aircraft on my radar. After some further directions, the next target was in sight – another Lancaster. After the first burst from us there was a small fire, and the machine dropped back its left wing and went down in a vertical dive. Shortly afterwards I saw it crash. It was some time between 2210 and 2215 hours. When it crashed there were heavy detonations; most probably it was the bomb load.

'After a short interval we again saw a Lancaster. After a long burst of fire the bomber caught fire and went down. I saw it crash some time between 2225 and 2230 hours. Immediately afterwards we saw yet another four-engined bomber: we were in the middle of the bomber stream. After one firing pass, this bomber went down in flames, at about 2240 hours. I saw the crash.

'Again I had a target on my search equipment. After a few corrections we again saw a Lancaster. There was one attack, and it caught fire in the fuselage. The fire started to go out, and we moved into position and Major Wittgenstein was ready to shoot when, in our own machine, there were terrible explosions and sparks. It immediately caught fire in the left wing, and began to go down. As I saw this the canopy above my head flew away, and I heard on the intercom a shout of *Raus!* Get out! I tore off my oxygen mask and helmet, and was then thrown out of the machine. After a short time I opened my parachute, and landed east of the Hohengöhrener Dam near Schönhausen.'

Wittgenstein's body was found in the wreckage the next day. He died with 83 night kills to his credit. His Ju 88 was probably shot down by one of the other bombers in the stream, thus avenging its fallen comrades.

As the new year progressed the Luftwaffe was able to strike heavier and heavier blows at the night raiders. On 28th January forty-three bombers were shot down out of 683 attacking Berlin, and the following month was even worse. On 15th February the Royal Air Force lost forty-two out of 891 striking at Berlin, and four days later seventy-eight out of 823 attacking Leipzig; in March, seventy-two bombers out of 811 despatched were lost during the attack on Berlin on the 24th. Even the successful British attack on Essen two days later, when out of 705 only nine were lost, was overshadowed by the appalling total cost.

The climax of this phase of the night bombing offensive came on 30th March 1944, when a force of 781 Lancasters and Halifaxes set out to attack Nuremburg. It was a moonlight night and the temperature was so low that the bombers streamed behind them dense white condensation trails – a comparatively rare phenomenon at the 18,000 to 20,000 altitudes flown by the British bombers. At the same time strong winds at that altitude caused the bomber stream to loose its cohesion, and the aircraft were scattered over a wide area. On this night the German ground fighter control organisation worked perfectly, and twenty-one *Gruppen* of 'Tame Boar' night fighters – about 200 aircraft – were scrambled. The outcome was a long running battle which ended in disaster for the British force: ninety-four bombers were shot down, and a further forty-six damaged.

Schweinfurt had marked a turning point in American bombing policy, now Nuremburg marked another for the British. The night bomber force temporarily ceased its deep penetration attacks on the German cities, and instead – as had been previously planned – began the systematic wrecking of the communications system in western Europe in preparation for the forthcoming invasion.

We left the American strategic bomber force in mid-October 1943, when it was still smarting after the blow it had suffered during the Schweinfurt attack. At the turn of the year it seemed to some Germans that they might be over the worst regarding the defence of their homeland: the American daylight offensive had been fought to a standstill, and the British night raiders were suffering heavier and heavier losses. But the first month of the new year brought the optimists back to ugly reality; they had not seen the end of the big daylight attacks, merely the end of the first phase. The American

answer to the German fighter defences was the same as that tried by the Luftwaffe during the battle over Britain back in 1940: the escort fighter. By carrying large droppable fuel tanks, Republic P-47 Thunderbolt and North American P-51 Mustang single-engined machines possessed the range to go with the bomber formations deep into enemy territory. And, unlike the Bf 110 over Britain, the American escort fighters were no lame ducks compared with their adversaries. Indeed, the P-51 was able to outperform all comers. The drop tanks cut its top speed by 35 mph, but once these had been released the fighter was more than 50 mph faster than the heavily-armed bomber-destroying versions of the Bf 109 and the Fw 190 which opposed it. The Thunderbolt was slightly less handy than the Mustang, but its strength and ability to absorb punishment were legendary.

In January, escort fighters accompanied B-17s as far as Münster and Kiel; by March P-51s with two 75-gallon drop tanks were able to fly to Berlin and back; later, with a

A Messerschmitt 410 heavy fighter breaks past a B-17 after a firing pass; the former carries a 50mm cannon under its nose

pair of 108-gallon drop tanks, the Mustang had a radius of action of 850 miles – sufficient to take in almost any target in German occupied Europe.

The effect of all this on the German defences was immediate and devastating. Oberleutnant Heinz Knocke, who flew Bf 109s with *II/JG 11*, later wrote: 'The bomber-alley lies about 6,000 feet below us – 600 to 800 of the heavy bombers are heading eastwards. Alongside and above them range the escorting fighters.

'And now I am utterly absorbed in the excitement of the chase. Specht dips his left wing-tip, and we peel off for the attack. Messerschmitt after Messerschmitt follows him down.

' "After them!" The radio is a babel of sound, with everybody shouting at once.

'I check my guns and adjust the sights as we dive down upon the

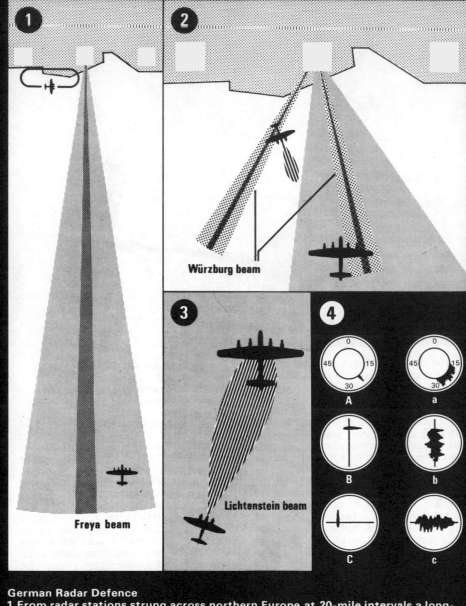

German Radar Defence
1 From radar stations strung across northern Europe at 20-mile intervals a long-range, early warning radar *Freya* would pick up the bomber. 2 As it closed, one short-range narrow-beam giant *Würzburg* set would fix on the bomber and another on the night fighter orbiting the station. The fighter would then be guided towards the bomber until 3 the fighters *Lichtenstein* radar made contact with its quarry. 4 ABC *Würtzburg* screens. B and C show elevation and bearing; when both 'blips' are central the radar is fixed on target. abc The effect on the signal of 'Window' — clouds of aluminium foil strip dropped from Allied aircraft

target. Then I grasp the stick with both hands, groping for the triggers with my right thumb and forefinger. I glance behind. The Thunderbolts are coming down after us.

'We are faster, and before they can intercept us we reach the Fortresses. Our fighters come sweeping through the bomber formation in a frontal attack. I press the triggers, and my aircraft shudders under the recoil.

' "After them!"

'My cannon shells punch holes in the wing of the Fortress. Blast! I had been aiming at the cabin.

'I climb away steeply behind the formation, followed by my flight. Then the Thunderbolts are upon us. It is a wild dogfight. Several times I try to manoeuvre into position for firing at one of their planes. Every time I am forced to break away, because there are two – four – five – or even ten Thunderbolts on my tail.'

Commanded by Major-General William Kepner, the American escort fighters became more and more aggressive with each month that passed. Kepner did not force his pilots to remain in the immediate vicinity of the bombers, but instead he allowed his junior commanders in the air to use their discretion on whether or not to pursue the German fighters who attempted to break off combat.

As more and more escort fighters became available, the situation became disastrous for the Luftwaffe. The first to suffer heavily were the twin-engined fighter units. For example, on 16th March forty-three Bf 110s of the *III/ZG 76* ran in for a massed attack on a formation of B-17s near Augsburg. But before the Germans could open fire, the Mustang escort struck. In the one-sided battle that followed several of the Messerschmitts were shot down right away, and the remainder were hounded all the way back to their base; in all, twenty-six of the German fighters were destroyed. Soon the German twin-engined fighters were forced to cease daylight operations against the bombers altogether.

Before the introduction of the American escorts, the Germans had devoted much energy to increasing the hitting-power of their single-engined fighters, so that they might more easily destroy the strongly-built American bombers. But the extra armament meant extra weight, and now this placed the defending pilots in an unenviable position if they had to engage in dogfights with the American escorts. Generalmajor Adolf Galland, the German fighter commander, tried to overcome this problem by forming seperate 'heavy' and 'light' fighter *Gruppen;* the former were equipped with Bf 109s and Fw 190s fitted with heavy batteries of cannon, and were to attack the bombers, the latter flew lightly armed Bf 109s and were to fight off the escorts. But these tactics were not a success: the Americans were often present in such numbers that they were able to cut through the German escort and do great execution to the 'heavy' fighter units.

In April 1944 Galland was forced to report to his superiors: 'Between January and April 1944 our day fighter arm lost more than 1,000 pilots. They included our best *Staffel, Gruppe* and *Geschwader* commanders. Each incursion by the enemy is costing us about fifty aircrew. The time has come when our force is within sight of collapse.' The Germans were beginning to lose the control of the air over their own country.

So it was that the renewed American daylight attacks on German industry were able to smash not only the targets, but also the German fighter force. For the Luftwaffe the only real answer to the problem of the escorts was the Me 262 jet fighter, for only this machine was fast enough to evade the American fighters. But Hitler had ordered that the initial production batches were all to be used as fighter-bombers, and the need to modify the airframe to enable bombs to be carried had delayed production by several months. The result was that in the early summer of 1944 there were very few of these jet aircraft available for anything. The great disaster, which Jeschonnek had shot himself rather than see, was coming to pass.

The renewed attack on England

The powerful Anglo-American bombing attacks on Germany brought enraged demands from Hitler for retaliatory attacks on British cities. Accordingly, on 3rd December 1943, Göring signalled Generalmajor Dietrich Peltz, his bomber commander in the west, that: 'To avenge the terror attacks of the enemy I have decided to intensify the air war over the British Isles, by means of concentrated attacks on cities, especially industrial centres and ports.'

The enterprise was given the codename 'Operation *Steinbock*' (Ibex). By the beginning of 1944 the Germans had collected a force of nearly 400 medium and heavy bombers in the west, Ju 88s, Ju 188s and Do 217s, Me 410s and He 117s (this type had been put into service even though the problem of the engine fires had not yet been cured). In addition there was a fighter-bomber unit, *SKG 10* with Fw 190s.

Peltz opened his attack on the British capital on the night of 21st January 1944, at the same time as the Royal Air Force was striking at Magdeburg. The German bombers attacked in two separate and compact waves, together involving 447 aircraft. In the face of the strong British defences, the attacking force suffered heavy losses and achieved little. A repeat attack by 285 aircraft on London on 29th January fared little better than the first, and the two raids together depleted Peltz's carefully husbanded strength by fifty-seven aircraft (7.8 per cent of the sorties flown).

During the Ibex operation Major Helmut Schmidt's I/KG 66, equipped with Ju 88s and Ju 188s, provided target marking for the rest of the force. The practice was for the first marking aircraft to arrive over the target at high level, often above 30,000 feet, a few minutes before the main force was due. The leading pathfinders would release flares over the objective, in the light of which other aircraft would go in a low level and drop distinctive white, green or yellow target marking bombs.

The Luftwaffe returned to London on seven nights in February, and on the 18th and 20th of that month made two well-concentrated attacks on the capital. From March onwards the focus of the attack shifted to include some of the ports where the invasion fleet was assembling, and Portsmouth, Plymouth and Weymouth, Bristol and Falmouth were all hit.

One may get an insight into how these attacks looked from the German side from the recollections of one of the Luftwaffe NCOs who took part in some of them, Gefreiter Rudi Prasse. Prasse flew on several of the Ibex operations as navigator/bomb-aimer on a Ju 188 of *KG 2*. Here he describes his part in the ninety-one aircraft attack on Bristol on the night of the 13th/14th May. The Ju 188 took off from Vannes in Brittany at 0030 hours, with Feldwebel Hans Engelke at the controls; it carried a load of two 2,200-pound and two 100-pound bombs:

'20,000 feet. Now we climb at 600 feet per minute, with the airspeed steady at 310 mph. In front of us there emerges a dark outline: the English coast. Now there is nothing of the defences to be seen, the long arms of the searchlight beams do not grope out for us. But we know that now, ten minutes before we cross the English coast, the enemy is getting ready for us. Now the first sirens are sounding in the coastal towns and on the airfields the first night fighters are already taking off. Hans begins to jink the aircraft – turning, climbing, diving – for nothing is more dangerous than holding a straight course for too long.

'As we cross the coast the first searchlight beams flash on; two, four, five beams grope after us, searching. Behind us are many more, certainly about fifty: this is the famous English coastal searchlight belt. Then we are through it, and it is dark again. Before us lies Bristol, our target.

'We arrive at the outskirts at 24,000 feet. Suddenly two great tentacles of light swing across the sky to flood the cabin with dazzling white light, forcing us to screw up our blinded eyes. We are being coned by two searchlights, which now follow us. "Put the jammer on," shouts Hans [the bomber carried a radar jamming transmitter, to counter the British searchlight control sets]. I hold my map against the nose so that the pilot can see his instruments. We dive through 1,000 feet turning steeply to the left, then fly straight ahead. The two searchlights, which have been joined by a further two, hunt the sky for us but we are once more in the darkness. "Heavy flak coming up" calls Erich [the underneath gunner], and Hans immediately changes course. There, above us at 26,000 feet, the first eight shells burst.

'More searchlights cut across the sky, and the flak bursts multiply. The dance has begun! The pilot flies uncommonly well, improvising a regular aerobatic programme before our eyes.

'To the left and below us a flaming red torch goes down. I note in my log: "Aircraft shot down at 0042 hours southwest of Bristol."

'0045 hours! The first flares blossom in rows over the city, lighting the targets with a dazzling white light. Over them hang the rows of green target markers, which float down slowly. On the ground the flak gunners concentrate their fire on the markers in an attempt to shoot them out. But it is too late. On the city heavy bombs are now bursting, and dark red fires rise into the sky.

'One short glance at the map – that must be the harbour there. I nudge Hans and point to the right: "We will attack!"

'Bomb doors open, switches on!

'There is a small jerk as our bombs fall away.

'Bomb doors closed!

'Our Dora, lighter by more than two tons, obeys its pilot and sweeps round in a steep left turn, on to a south-easterly course away from the target. Soon we are clear.'

The Junkers 188 landed back at Vannes at 0305 hours, without further incident.

From British records we now know that the attack – which cost the Luftwaffe six bombers – was not so successful as it had appeared to Prasse. Of the eighty-three tons of bombs recorded as having landed on English soil that night only a paltry three tons fell within the city limits of Bristol. By 1944 the British fire decoy organisation had become very efficient.

The Ibex operations petered out at the end of May 1944, and the units involved sat back to lick their wounds. But the resting time was to be short indeed, for early in June the Allied forces landed on the north coast of France, at Normandy. The losses suffered by the German bomber force over Britain had been serious enough, but they were as nothing compared with those now in store for it.

Heinkel 177 bomber

Messerschmitt 410 bomber

The second battle of France

By the spring of 1944 it was quite clear to the Germans that the Allied invasion of north-western Europe could not be long delayed. But in spite of this, the intense pressure on the Russian front, coupled with the home defence commitment, made it impossible to move in the units previously allocated to meet the threat. For example, in the east a force of 550 ground attack aircraft had to be held back in anticipation of a major Russian offensive; as a result General-feldmarschall Sperrle's *Luftflotte III* in the west was able to muster a ground attack force somewhat smaller than that which had been employed – and ineffectively at that – to counter the Salerno landings.

On 5th June, the day before the American and British troops landed in Normandy, *Luftflotte III* comprised 810 aircraft:
The weakness in tactical reconnaissance types was particularly serious, for there were only twenty-five aircraft in this category. The most potent part of the force was the 200-aircraft strong anti-shipping unit, *Fliegerkorps X*, based in the south of France. Its machines, each equipped to carry either the Hs 293 and Fritz X guided weapons, or torpedoes, were intended to spearhead the attack on the initial and reinforcing waves. In particular, the missile-carrying He 177s of *KG 40* were expected to achieve great things, and morale within the unit was very high indeed.

On the first day of the invasion the combined Allied air forces operated with a strength of more than 3,000 bombers and 5,000 fighters and fighter-bombers. *Luftflotte III* was utterly swamped; when units tried to penetrate to the bridgehead area they were cut to pieces by the defending fighters, and it soon became clear that daylight anti-shipping operations were quite out of the question. When *Fliegerkorps X* did attempt to strike at the concentrations of ships at night it suffered heavy losses from both night fighters and anti-aircraft fire, and by the adroit use of smokescreens the Allied escorts prevented the effective use of guided weapons. During the ten days following the invasion, only five ships were lost to direct air attack.

As soon as the first British and American troops landed the Germans implemented their previously planned reinforcement arrangements, and aircraft were flown in from other theatres. By 10th June 300 fighters and 135 bombers had arrived from Germany and Italy; as a result, *Luftflotte III* was able to put up a force of over 1,000 combat aircraft against the invaders. This was the strongest that the force was ever to become, but even so it left the German airmen outnumbered by something of the order of eight to one. For a time the Luftwaffe did try to use interceptor units transfered straight from the defence of Germany in the ground-attack role, in an effort to overcome the crippling shortage of specialised aircraft for this work. But because the German pilots involved were quite untrained in attacking ground targets the results obtained did not justify the heavy losses suffered. Moreover, the available fighter force had to be cut still further by the need to provide escorts.

So it was that the finely-laid German plans, to use vast numbers of ground attack aircraft to destroy the Allied forces as they came ashore, came to nothing. Moreover, the powerful American and British attacks on the German rear areas quickly hurled the Luftwaffe on to the defensive, forcing it to expand much of its effort to protect its own installations. The hard-pressed German ground troops had to fend for themselves. And because of the delays in the Me 262 programme, while the aircraft was being modified into a fighter-bomber, jet aircraft were nowhere to be seen.

Meanwhile, at sea, the strength of the day and night defences forced the Germans to give up the idea of attacking the shipping with missiles and torpedoes. Instead, they began to concentrate their efforts on sowing mines in the shallow waters through which the Allied vessels had to pass. By the end of July the Luftwaffe had flown more than 1,500 sorties to this end, and had laid between 3,000 and 4,000 mines of all types. For the Allies the campaign caused considerable inconvenience, for the newly-developed German pressure mines proved to be extremely difficult to sweep and could be countered only by restricting all movement to a snail's pace while the ships were in shallow water. By the end of July mines had caused the loss of seven destroyers, two minesweepers, and seventeen merchantment and auxiliary vessels. Although the cumulative effect was great, and did cause difficulties and delays, these Luftwaffe operations could never have been decisive. The most the Germans could hope for was to retard the Allied build-up ashore; having regard to the weakness of *Luftflotte III*, it was probably the only way that it could have operated to any effect.

Throughout June and July the Luftwaffe struggled manfully with the problem of challenging the almost complete Allied air superiority in the west, but without success.

The airfields used by the Luftwaffe in the west suffered the full weight of the Allied bomber force, and attacks were repeated again and again on the more important bases in order to keep them out of action.

With the British and American forces established in growing strength in Northern France, the Germans found it impossible to contain them inside the Normandy bridgehead. At the end of July the American forces on the Allied right flank smashed their way through the German defensive line, and began to advance down the western edge of the Cherbourg peninsula. At its southern end are the villages of Avranches and Pontaubault, and there the bridges over the river See and Sélune. In their rush southwards the Americans seized both bridges intact and General Patton, realising his heaven-sent opportunity, poured his men across. Of the incident, the famous historian Chester Wilmot later wrote: 'Patton did not wait to draw up movement plans or march tables. The bottleneck of the single road from Avranches to Pontaubault became a sheep-race. At the mouth senior officers herded units through in any order. At the exit each division was allocated one of the roads radiating from Pontaubault and, as its units came through the race, they were drafted down the appropriate route . . . Defying field regulations and textbook rules, Patton moved seven divisions down this one road in 72 hours.' Once through this bottleneck the American armoured units fanned out, the majority swinging to the east in a devastatingly powerful right hook that was soon to catch two army groups in the Falaise pocket.

The Avranches and Pontaubault bridges were, as both sides saw clearly, the key to the land battle. *Luftflotte III* made a considerable effort against them, including Do 217s carrying Hs 293 glider bombs – the first time these weapons were used against ground targets. But the British and American night fighters beat off the raiders, and the attempts to smash the bridges were unsuccessful.

August 1944 was taken up with the headlong retreat of the German forces out of France. The Luftwaffe fighter commander, in the west, General Bülowins, made strenuous efforts to maintain some sort of presence in the air; but this became more and more difficult as the various units were forced to pull back to bases in Holland and Germany. By the middle of September the Germans had been ejected from virtually the whole of France and Belgium. The second Battle of France was over, and the Luftwaffe had been able to play little part in it. But even while the battle had been in progress, the Germans were making one last all-out attempt to smash the British capital.

The
robot
bombardment

The Fieseler Fi 103 or FZG 76, more familiarly known as the V1 (short for *Vergeltunsgwaffe 1* – retaliation weapon No 1), was a small pilotless aircraft with a wing span of 17.7 feet and a length of nearly 25.4 feet. To save precious aluminium, pressed steel was used in its construction wherever possible; the machine weighed a little over two tons, of which 1,870 pounds of high explosive made up the warhead. The power unit was a single Argus pulse-jet engine, developing 740 pounds of thrust and with an operational life of about half an hour. After being catapulted off the ground, the missile accelerated up to its cruising speed of about 400 mph at a height of about 3,000 feet – too low for the heavy anti-aircraft guns to operate at their most effective, and too high for the lighter guns.

The Fi 103 made its first powered flight in December 1942. By the middle of 1943 it had flown a distance of 152 miles, and impacted within half a mile of its target (this was an exceptionally accurate shot). This success gave the Luftwaffe High Command considerable encouragement, and the weapon was

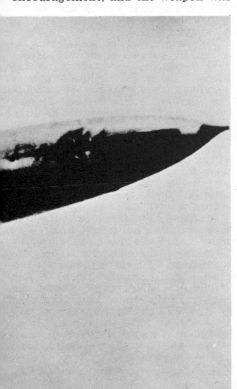

placed in full production – such a range was quite sufficient for the bombardment of London from the Pas de Calais. In parallel with the Fi 103, and also for the purpose of striking at the British capital, the Germans developed the A-4 rocket (generally known as the V2); the A-4 was, however, an army and not a Luftwaffe project, and thus falls outside the compass of this volume.

The 'Flak' arm of the Luftwaffe assumed responsibility for the operation of the Fi 103, and Oberst Max Wachtel's *Flak Regiment 155(W)* was formed specially for the purpose. While the regiment was under training at Zempin on the Baltic in the autumn of 1943, 40,000 workers of the Todt organisation were engaged in the task of constructing a total of sixty-four main and thirty-two reserve catapult sites. Most of them were aligned on London.

The provisional date set for the opening of the flying-bomb attack on London was December 1943, but the production schedule had slipped badly and the necessary flying bombs were not available. Moreover, the large and conspicuous catapult launchers had not escaped the notice of the ever watchful British Intelligence service, which had followed the construction work with interest. Now the Allied air forces struck out. In a series of intensive bombing attacks the majority of the sites were either completely wrecked or else severely damaged; attempts to repair the launchers brought only repeat attacks.

After this disaster the Germans were forced to devise a new type of launching ramp, a ramp much simpler and less conspicuous than the earlier one had been; forewarned of what they could expect if there was any lapse, the men of *Flakregiment 155(W)* observed the strictest security precautions at the new sites, and camouflage was elaborate.

By April 1944, the flying bombs were at last becoming available in useful numbers, and the modified ramps were also ready. But by now the Allied pre-invasion attacks on communications targets in France and

Fiesler Fi 103 Flying Bomb

141

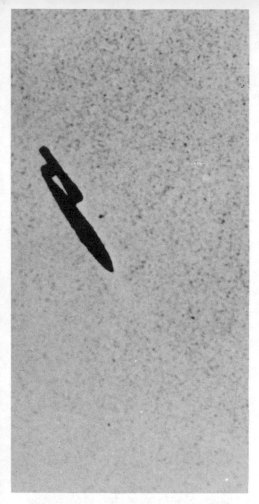

was so great that Lord Cherwell, Mr Churchill's scientific adviser, commented: 'The mountain hath groaned, and given forth a mouse!'

There was a delay of three days, while the Germans reorganised themselves, then the bombardment began in earnest with a firing rate of between 120 and 190 missiles per day. This rate was kept up until the latter part of August, when one by one the firing sites were captured by the advancing Allied ground troops. At 0400 on the morning of 1st September the initial phase of the attack came to an end, after 8,617 flying bombs had been launched at London.

Supplementing the ground-launched flying bombs during the attack was the He 111 unit *III KG 3;* the *Gruppe* had had its aircraft modified to carry a single flying bomb between the starboard engine and the fuselage, and aircraft now fired the missiles while airborne, at London, Southampton and Gloucester. But the accuracy of this method of bombardment left very much to be desired; in the case of the attack on Southampton the British found flying-bomb craters all over the countryside, and took it to be an unsuccessful attempt to strike at Portsmouth!

The weight and drag penalty of the externally-carried missile imposed a severe performance penalty on the already outmoded Heinkels, and to survive in the face of the overwhelming British defences the German crews were forced to operate at night and at low level. The bombers would make their approach flights low down over the sea at 300 feet, below the cover of the British radar screen, and make a brief 'pop up' to 1,500 feet when some forty miles from the target to fire the missile. Then the bombers would return to their bases at low level.

In September 1944 the worsening military situation forced *III/KG 3* to move from Holland back into western Germany, where it continued its operations from the airfields at Aalhorn, Varelbusch, Zwischenahn and Handorf-bei-Münster. Meanwhile, the capture of the ground launching sites in the Pas de Calais gave a new importance to the air-launched bombardment. *III/KG 3* was re-designated *I/KG 53*, and by November 1944 this and

Belgium had got under way, and these greatly increased the difficulties of moving anything into the area.

By the beginning of June 1944, six months later than the date originally planned, the Luftwaffe was almost, but not quite, ready to launch its robot attack. There were still the final preparations to be completed when the American and British troops landed in Normandy; now this work was given a new impetus.

On the night of 12th June, the first salvo of flying bombs was fired at London. It was to have been a grand affair, but so many sites reported that they were unserviceable that only ten of the bombs were actually fired; of these four reached England, and only one hit the capital. The anti-climax the newly converted Second and Third *Gruppen* of the *Geschwader* were operating in the stand-off bombing role.

Between a third and a half of the Fi 103s launched from the air failed to function correctly and, as we have seen, the accuracy of the remainder was poor. Just before dawn on 16th September 1944, for example, fifteen Heinkels launched their missiles at London from firing positions off the east coast of England. Nine Fi 103s got under way satisfactorily, of which three were destroyed by British ships and aircraft before they could cross the coast, and two more were shot down by fighters over land. Of the remaining four, two fell in open countryside in Essex. Only two reached the sprawling London area, a target roughly fifteen miles in radius; one hit Woolwich, the other Barking. Such was the effort necessary for the Luftwaffe to deliver just one and a half tons of explosive on the British capital by this method.

Most of the flying bombs were aimed at targets in southern England, though from time to time cities in the north did come under attack. Just before dawn on 24th December 1944 some fifty Heinkels of *KG 53* fired their bombs at Manchester, from launch points just off the east coast of England, between Skegness and Bridlington. Thirty bombs crossed the coast, and proceeded westwards towards their target. Eleven of the bombs fell within fifteen miles of the city, six landed within ten miles of it, but only one of the Fi 103s impacted within the city limits of Manchester. One of the launching He 111s was shot down by an RAF night fighter.

As might be expected, the Royal Air Force's reaction to these stand-off attacks was vigorous. But the low-flying Heinkels proved to be difficult targets. When attacked, the German pilots would reduce speed almost to the stall, get down as low as they possibly could, and turn into their assailants.

On 10th January 1945 *KG 53* had 101 He 111s on strength. Four days later the unit ceased operations, mainly because of the crippling fuel shortage. From first to last the stand-off bombing force had lost seventy-seven

Heinkels, sixteen of them to night fighters and the remainder in accidents largely attributable to the hazardous nature of the work.

In the meantime the Germans were able to resume the bombardment of London from ground launching sites in Holland, using an improved longer-range version of the Fi 103. This final phase of the attack lasted until 30th March 1945, and when it ended a total of about 275 bombs had been fired from the Dutch ramps by the SS; but by now the fighter and gun defences had reached such a fine peak of efficiency that only thirteen of these reached the London area.

All in all, about 10,500 Fi 103s were fired at England; the great majority, about eighty-five per cent, were fired from ground catapults. Of the total, 7,488 crossed the British coast or were otherwise observed by the defences, and 3,957 were shot down before they could get through to their targets. Of the 3,531 which eluded the defences, 2,419 reached London, about thirty reached Southampton and Portsmouth, and one hit Manchester. Thus approximately three quarters of the ground-launched bombs failed to get to their targets for one reason or another; of the air-launched bombs the figure was nine tenths. Those bombs that did get through caused the death of 6,184 civilians: an average of roughly three deaths for every five bombs fired. A further 17,981 people were injured.

Thus ended the flying bomb attack. Had it been possible to co-ordinate it with the manned bomber raids in January 1944 – and the Germans had hoped to do this– the British defences would have been seriously over-extended, and large areas of the capital might possibly have suffered damage. But as it was, the defences were able to take on one threat at a time, and effectively countered both. Finally, the advancing Allied troops captured the ground launching sites in the Pas de Calais, and for the Londoners the worst was over. True, the flying bombs were still to fall on the capital at irregular intervals for the next seven months. But both sides knew that this desultory effort was not going to change the course of the war one bit.

Oil:
the
Achilles
heel

The oil refinery at Bohlen, shortly
after an attack by the RAF

Before considering the German position regarding fuel in 1944, it is necessary to take a brief look at the state of affairs up to that time. Even as late as 1939 the production of high octane aviation petrol had fallen far short of what was anticipated to be necessary for a full-scale war. So for the last two years of peace the Germans had imported large stocks, and accumulated a reserve of more than 350,000 tons – enough for three months of intensive air operations, even if home production was to fail completely.

However, the speed of the initial campaigns in Poland, Norway and France, and later in the Balkans and Greece, coupled with the capture of stocks of fuel in these countries, meant that there was little call on the reserves. Immediately prior to the Russian campaign there was a slight cutback in flying to allow stocks to build up further, but otherwise there was no shortage of fuel during the early part of the war.

For the first year of the Russian campaign the Luftwaffe was able to operate without restriction, though there were sometimes local fuel shortages due to transport difficulties in the forward areas. But during the second year the intensive operations resulted in a far heavier consumption of aviation fuel. By September 1942 the Germans had reached crisis point, with stocks down to two weeks' supply. Moreover, because of the crucial position on the Eastern and the Mediterranean Fronts, there could be no cutting back on the level of consumption there. The result was a drastic pruning in other areas, with operations in the west cut to a minimum and a greatly reduced fuel quota for the flying training schools. Fuel supplies to aircraft and engine manufacturers were also cut right back; this had the result that only one aircraft in five received a full flight check after it left the assembly line – the remainder were flown for about twenty minutes, then shipped direct to the front-line units.

Reichsminister Albert Speer realised full well the significance of the fuel shortage, and by the late summer of 1943 his sweeping reorganisation of the industry began to bear fruit as the synthetic fuel plants raised production by leaps and bounds. Stocks steadily rose, to nearly 400,000 tons by December 1943 and a record 574,000 tons by April 1944.

This, then, was the position in May 1944, when the American strategic bombers began to concentrate their efforts against the German oil producing centres. In June the Royal Air Force joined them for now, by routing the night bombers in over France, where after the invasion the German air reporting organisation was rapidly approaching collapse, it was possible to avoid the worst effects of the defences; moreover the night raiders now had their own 'escorts', in the shape of the specially-equipped radar and radio jamming aircraft which accompanied them as they penetrated the defences.

The effect of the combined Allied air offensive against the German oil industry was devastating. By 22nd June production had fallen by about ninety per cent, and the production of aviation fuel for that month was only 52,000 tons compared with 195,000 tons in May. As the attacks continued, things went from bad to worse: in July only 35,000 tons were produced, in August 16,000, and in September a paltry 7,000 tons. Now the Luftwaffe was living on its fat, on the reserve accumulated during the winter and the spring. As a result it was not until August 1944 that the flying units began to feel the full force of the crisis in fuel supply.

The fuel famine cut short many cherished German dreams. Not the least of· these was the full *Geschwader* of long-range four-engined bombers, which had just been assembled under great secrecy. The unit was *Kampgeschwader 1*, commanded by Oberstleutnant Horst von Riesen, and it was equipped with some ninety He 177 heavy bombers. During May and June 1944 the *Geschwader* had moved to its operational bases in East Prussia, and begun operations against the Russians.

Even before the famine, fuel supplies had always been a difficult matter so far as *KG 1* was concerned. There was no reserve of fuel at the airfields, and as the specially allocated fuel trains arrived the bombers were fuelled up ready for action. This hand-to-mouth existence imposed serious limitations on Riesen's force: on one occasion enemy fighter-bombers had caught the vital train, and not a drop of fuel arrived; as a result the operations planned for the following day had to be cancelled.

Each He 177 required about six tons of fuel for a medium range operation, so for an eighty-aircraft attack *KG 1* needed 490 tons. But during the month of August 1944 this 490 tons represented an average day's output of aviation fuel by the *entire* German industry! There could be no arguing with the simple arithmetic: there just was no fuel to keep the heavy bombers going. The men of *KG 1* were ordered to take their machines back to airfields in central Germany, where this and many other famous bomber units were disbanded. It is ironic that the He 177s should have had to be withdrawn from operations for this reason, at the very moment when this type of bomber was achieving the success which had eluded it for so long.

The bomber units were not the only ones to suffer. Most of the flying training schools were shut down, and their partially-trained pilots were drafted into the infantry. Reconnaissance flights were severely limited, and fighter-bomber support was permitted only in 'decisive situations'. During the late summer of 1944 fighter operations in defence of targets in Germany were allowed to continue without restriction, but later even these were cut back. Only the units equipped with jet aircraft escaped the effects of the famine, for these machines ran on low grade petrol which was available in relative abundance.

Under Hitler's watchful eye, Reichsminister Speer took the most energetic action to repair the hydro-generation plants, where the *ersatz* petrol was made, and to prevent their further destruction. Seven thousand engineers were released from the army to assist with the reconstruction, and an unlimited supply of slave labour was placed at his disposal. Concrete blast walls were built round the more vulnerable parts of the refineries, and smoke generators were

German aircraft production reached new heights during 1944, but due to the fuel famine many of the aircraft remained on the ground

moved into position to screen the plants during attacks. Large numbers of heavy anti-aircraft guns were moved in from other areas for the defence of the plants, so that they became veritable fortresses, *Hydriesfestungen*. At the plants themselves deep shelters were built so that the workers could resume work at the earliest possible moment after an attack. Finally, to ensure that morale at the plants did not flag, their workers came under the 'special supervision' of the SS.

By the use of such draconian measures, the German synthetic oil industry was able to recover a little from the pounding it had suffered in the summer. The plants were gradually brought back into operation, and between attacks they were able to produce useful quantities of fuel; in October 19,000 tons was produced, and in November 39,000 tons. Used astutely, this was to be enough to inject, temporarily, a new life into the otherwise almost paralysed Luftwaffe.

The death of an air force

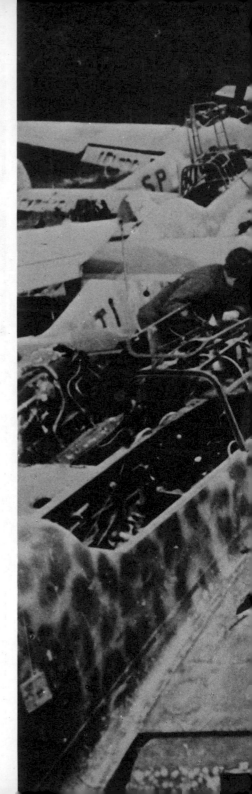

During the late autumn of 1944 the Eastern and Western Fronts quietened, as Germany's enemies stopped to draw breath after their successful summer offensives. The year had seen a series of massive defeats for German arms, on all fronts and in all three dimensions. Clearly the days of the Third Reich were numbered. But now, faced with the sole alternative of unconditional surrender, a course made the more hideous by imaginative propaganda, for the most part the men of the German armed forces resolved to fight on to the bitter end. As one saying in Germany at the time ran: 'Enjoy the war, because the peace will be dreadful.'

Never timid about launching attacks, Hitler saw that a powerful offensive now, when many thought that Germany was finished, would catch her enemies off balance. At the very least this would buy time, time desperately needed to introduce advanced types of jet aircraft into the Luftwaffe and potent new U-boats into the Navy. It was with this in mind that Hitler had his generals plan Operation 'Wacht am Rhein' (Watch on the Rhine): a force of 200,000 men, including seven Panzer divisions, was to smash its way through the weakly-held Ardennes sector of the US front, and thrust on to the vitally important supply port of Antwerp, more than eighty miles away.

To cover the offensive, the Luftwaffe assembled a powerful force of 2,460 aircraft:

LEVEL BOMBERS	55
JET BOMBERS	40
GROUND-ATTACK AIRCRAFT	390
SINGLE-ENGINED FIGHTERS	1,770
TWIN-ENGINED FIGHTERS	140
RECONNAISSANCE AIRCRAFT	65

And, as we have seen, the newly-repaired oil plants had been able to produce sufficient fuel to enable the force to go into action, for a short time at least.

The Luftwaffe was to perform a twofold task during the offensive. Firstly, it was to knock out the opposing air forces by means of a large-scale surprise attack on their airfields, and after that an umbrella of German fighters was to seal off the battle zone. Secondly, once air superiority had thus been gained, the German ground attack units were to support the advancing troops, while the longer-range bomber and night ground-attack Gruppen were to strike at the enemy rear areas.

The attack on the Allied airfields, code-named Operation 'Bodenplatte' (Ground Plate), was intended to preceed the offensive on the ground. By mid-December all the planning was complete, and the various units were in position. As in all matters concerned with the new offensive, security precautions were elaborate – and successful. On 14th December the commanders of the fighter and ground attack Gruppen earmarked for 'Ground Plate' were summoned to the headquarters of Jagdkorps II near Altenkirchen. There the surprised men were briefed on what was expected of them by the energetic Generalmajor Dietrich Peltz, who had recently been appointed to command the Jagdkorps and was responsible for the operation. Peltz told his audience of the plan to attack, simultaneously, the Allied airfields at Volkel, Eindhoven, Antwerp/Deurne, Le Culot, St Trond, Metz/Frascaty, those in the Brussels area and those in the Ghent area. It was hoped that well over 1,000 aircraft would be available for the operation. The operation was then discussed, and points of detail agreed upon. There were to be three executive code-words: 'Varus' – meaning that the operation was to take place, and followed by a number which indicated the date; 'Teutonicus' – authority for the detailed briefing of all crewmen taking part, and the arming of the aircraft with special loads if necessary; and 'Hermann' – given with a number, which indicated the time when all the raiding forces were to be over their targets.

The great German offensive opened on the morning of 16th December 1944, but without the planned strike on the Allied airfields: thick fog during this and for most of the eight days which followed put a virtual stop to air operations by either side. Meanwhile, German troops made substantial gains on the ground. On 17th December the cloud lifted a little, and the Luftwaffe ground attack units flew some 600 sorties, for the most

Me 163 rocket fighter

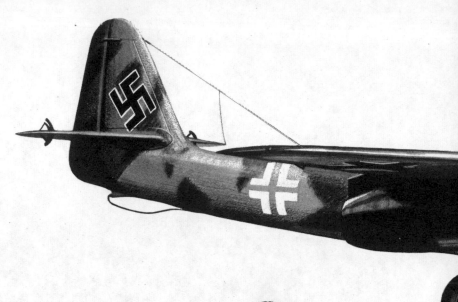

Messerschmitt Me 262

Engines: Two Junkers Jumo 004 turbojets, each developing 1,980 pounds of thrust. *Armament:* four 30 mm cannon, and twenty-four 55 mm R4M air-to-air rockets. *Maximum speed:* 540 mph at 20,000 feet. *Rate of climb:* 3,937 feet per minute at sea level. *Range:* 652 miles at 30,000 feet. *Ceiling:* 37,500 feet. *Weights:* empty, 9,741 pounds; loaded, 14,101 pounds. *Span:* 40 feet 11½ inches. *Length:* 34 feet 9½ inches.

The Arado 234
Engines: Two Junkers Jumo 004 turbojets, 1,980 lbs thrust.
Armament: up to 3,300 pounds of bombs and two 20mm cannon.
Maximum speed: 461 mph at 20,000 feet. *Range:* 684 miles with 3,300 lbs bombs.
Ceiling: 32,810 feet. *Weight: empty/loaded:* 11,464 lbs/21,715 lbs.
Span: 46 feet 3½ inches. *Length:* 41 feet 5½ inches

part ground strafing missions; when night fell bombers and fighters flew a further 300 sorties, against reinforcements moving up in the Allied rear. Gradually, however, American resistance on the ground stiffened, as hardened combat units from other parts of France moved into the area. By 20th December the spearheads of the German attack, which had in places advanced nearly fifty miles since the beginning of the offensive, were forced to a halt.

On 24th December the fog finally lifted, and now the Luftwaffe once more felt the weight of the Allied aerial strength: eleven of the more important airfields used to cover the Ardennes offensive were seriously damaged. On the following day, Christmas Day, the regrouped American ground troops went on to the offensive and started to squeeze the Germans out of 'The Bulge'.

During the two weeks following the Altenkirchen briefing, the 'Ground Plate' operation had faded into the background, as the units involved concerned themselves with other types of operation, mainly defensive. Many of the *Gruppen* commanders assumed that the airfield strike plan had been shelved. Their surprise was all the greater, then, when the executive signal was flashed to the German fighter bases on the afternoon of 31st December: 'Execute Hermann 1.1.45, time 09.20 hours.' That evening, in their base operations rooms, the mass of German pilots first learned of the scope of the following day's operation, and of the parts they were to play in it. They saw their routes laid out on the wall charts, their turning points, and the compass headings to the targets. During the approach flights, which were to be made at tree-top height to avoid the radar, the pilots were ordered to observe strict radio silence; even if circumstances forced them to bail out or crash land, they were not to transmit.

The main briefing over, the 'Ground Plate' pilots were ordered to bed for an early night; if the British and Americans were going to occupy New Year's Eve 'making whoopee', some at least of their opponents had more serious matters to think about.

The date of the operation had been chosen for the Germans by the vagaries of the weather; but if the enemy's New Year hangovers could be exploited, then so much the better.

At 0500 hours on New Year's Day the German pilots were roused, received their final briefings, and changed into their flying kit. By 0900 hours the first aircraft were airborne, and making for their rendezvous points. In all, about 800 fighter-bombers, almost all of them Messerschmitt 109s and Focke Wulf 190s, got airborne; the force was not so large as the one originally planned, for the previous week's battles had taken their toll.

One of the most successful of the attacks was that on the airfield at Eindhoven, carried out by *I, II* and *IV/JG 3* – the unit which had been named after Udet. *I/JG 3* and *II/JG 3* were equipped with Messerschmitt 109s and were based at Paderborn and Lippspringe respectively; *IV/JG 3* was equipped with Fw 190s, and based at Gütersloh. The aircraft took off in sections of four in line abreast, with the section leader to port; section followed section in line astern. Thus formed up, the individual *Gruppen* made for the *Geschwader* rendezvous point over Lippstadt; from there the force of eighteen sections of four, seventy-two aircraft in all, flew westwards at heights of between sixty and 160 feet on an almost straight track to their target 140 miles away. The penultimate leg to the target ended at a point slightly to the north east of Eindhoven airfield, and at this turning point for the run-in each section leader slid in front of his section of four.

Jagdgeschwader 3 hit Eindhoven just as the Typhoon fighter-bombers of Nos 438 and 439 Squadrons of the Royal Canadian Air Force were taxiing out for an operation of their own. As ordered, the German pilots attacked the aircraft on the ground with their cannon and machine guns; between each firing pass, the attackers circled the airfield in an anti-clockwise direction. British records state that the Messerschmitts and Focke Wulfs 'attacked the field in a well-organised manner, being persistent and well-led'. Within minutes both of the Canadian squadrons had had almost all their aircraft destroyed or seriously damaged, and other units at Eindhoven suffered heavily too.

Everywhere the 'Ground Plate' attackers achieved complete surprise but, unfortunately for the Germans, few of the attacks were as successful as that on Eindhoven had been. Indeed, the strikes on Volkel, Antwerp/Deurne and Le Culot were all conspicuous failures. Sometimes the formations failed to find their targets altogether, while at others there was great confusion over the objectives as the attacking aircraft got in each other's way.

The New Year's Day attack cost the Allied Air Forces 144 aircraft destroyed and a further sixty-two damaged beyond unit repair. To achieve this the Luftwaffe lost about 200 aircraft and almost as many pilots; of the 127 German aircraft which fell inside the British and American sectors that day, and which could be checked, forty-one had been shot down by fighters, eighty-two by anti-aircraft fire, and sixteen had fallen to other or unknown causes. To the Americans and British the 'Ground Plate' losses were serious, but they were almost all made good within two weeks.

So it was that the piston-engined fighter units of the Luftwaffe went out in a final blaze of glory. For the rest of the war they were to be able to take little part in the proceedings; the renewal of the Allied bombing attacks on the oil refineries in December had again strangled supplies of high grade aviation fuel, and the Ardennes offensive and the 'Ground Plate' attack had bitten deeply into the already-slender reserve.

For the German aircraft manufacturers the almost total lack of fuel was all the more disheartening because their year's efforts to step up production, in spite of powerful bombing attacks on the factories, had been an outstanding success: during 1944 they had produced 40,593 aircraft, more than they had in 1942 and 1943 put together. But of these aircraft only 1,041 were jet-propelled types, and the majority of the surviving of the remaining 39,552 piston-engined aircraft were now forced to sit on the ground for want of fuel.

The only German aircraft able to continue operating at will were the newly introduced jet aircraft, the Me 262 and the Arado 234. Both of these were available to the front-line units in such small numbers, however, that they had little more than a nuisance value against the Allied ground troops. For example, the Arado 234s of Major Robert Kowalewski's *KG 76* and the Me 262 bombers of Major Wolfgang Schenk's *KG 51* often flew singly against American troops in the Ardennes. The reaction to these pin-pricks was immediate and formidable: standing patrols at 5,000 feet, 10,000 and 15,000 feet, and when a jet showed up the American fighters would pounce on it. But the swift jet bombers proved to be very difficult targets, and German losses were few and far between. If this sort of bombing caused little damage, at least the 'decoy duck' tactics did succeed in tying down several American fighters which might otherwise have been attacking ground targets; it was the nearest thing to air cover the weary German troops were to get during the closing months of the war.

By September 1944 Hitler had begun to relent on the question of the use of the Me 262 as a fighter; during the *Führer Konferenz* held between the 21st and the 23rd of that month, the minutes recorded that Hitler had agreed that: 'The Ar 234 will, with all possible despatch, continue to be turned out as a bomber in the greatest possible numbers. As it is possible to use this aircraft for the short range targets with three 1,100 pound bombs, and for long range targets with one 1,100 pound bomb, under considerably more favourable general conditions than the [Me 262] when used as a bomber, the *Führer* confirms his earlier promise that, for every single battleworthy 234 accepted as a bomber, the General in charge of fighters will be allocated one battleworthy 262 fighter.'

As a result of this change of heart, some forty Me 262s were immediately formed into a fighter unit under the command of the Austrian fighter ace Major Walter Nowotny. The unit was designated *Kommando Novotny* after its leader, and had become operational early in October 1944 from the bases at Achmer and Hesepe near Osnabruck. In spite of some severe teething and maintenance troubles, the new jet fighter proved to be a great success against the US bomber formations; in the first month Nowotny's men claimed twenty-two victories, in spite of the low serviceability rate which only rarely allowed more than three or four aircraft per day for operations.

On 9th November 1944, just one month after his unit had begun operations, Nowotny himself was shot down and killed after being attacked by an Allied fighter while he was trying to land his Me 262 back at Achmer; in his memory the Me 262 fighter unit then being formed from *Kommando Novotny, Jagdgeschwader 7,* was also given his name. Commanded initially by Major Johannes Steinhoff, the Me 262s of *JG 7* played an increasingly important part in opposing the US day bomber attacks. But, as a result of transport and supply problems and competition with German fighter-bomber units for the available Me 262s, the *I* and *II/JG 7* never reached full strength.

Then, in January 1945, one more Me 262 fighter unit was formed: the elite *Jagdverband 44* (Fighter Unit 44). Commanded by the erstwhile head of the German fighter force, Generalleutnant Adolf Galland, *JV 44* soon numbered within its ranks many of the best of the surviving fighter aces. Highly decorated men like Oberst Günther Lutzow and Oberstleutnant Gerhard Barkhorn, both with the Knight's Cross with Swords and Oakleaves, Oberstleutnant Wolfgang Späte and Major Walter Krupinski, both with the Knight's Cross and Oakleaves, these and many others came to *JV 44* from positions of command because the other, piston-engined fighter, units lacked the fuel to get off the ground.

The men of *JG 7* and *JV 44* fought many spirited air battles during the closing months of the war. For example, on 19th March 1945, when 1,250 American heavy bombers with a strong fighter escort set out to attack Berlin, thirty-seven Me 262s

of the *I* and *II/JG 7* took off to intercept. That day the powerful raiding force lost twenty-four bombers and five fighters, most of them in air combat, but managed to shoot down only two of the sleek jets.

But such actions, disconcerting though they were to Germany's enemies, could do nothing to stem the tide of defeat which was sweeping over the country. Inexorably the tattered remnants of the Luftwaffe were squeezed up into Schleswig Holstein in the north and Bavaria in the south, as the invading armies from the east and the west met in the middle and sliced Germany into two. On 6th May Grossadmiral Karl Dönitz, who had inherited the leadership of the crumbling Third Reich from Hitler at the beginning of the month, ordered the remainder of his forces to lay down their arms the next day. The war in Europe was over.

The atmosphere in the Luftwaffe at the end is well summed up by one of the German pilots, who was at the airfield at Leck in Schleswig Holstein. He wrote in his diary: '6th May 1945. We lined up the airvehicles and ground equipment in parade order. The English were astonished at the imposing scene at the airfield: a view of more than a hundred aircraft, standing with a pride born of sadness. The newer types, the Me 262s and the He 162s, which had hardly begun operations, stood between the well-blooded Bf 109s and Fw 190s, victors in thousands of air battles; all of these were to be handed over to the enemy. 7th May 1945. We have removed the propellers, rudders and guns from the aircraft. For us pilots the sight at the airfield is indescribably sad and painful. Our pride, our air force, our world, forced to be placed on exhibition, naked. At least thirty or forty Me 262s, the fastest fighters in the world, stand nose by nose next to each other, ready to be handed over.'

Now Germany's conquerors set about the task of dismantling the air force which, in its heyday, had been the terror of Europe. For the men, there were the prison cages. For a few of the aircraft, those which were new or those which were interesting, there were places at the

various proving grounds of the victors; but for the great majority of aircraft there was only the scrapheap. A few installations, those which might be of some use to the occupying powers, were kept on; the rest were destroyed.

The Luftwaffe had fought bravely, to its last drop of fuel if not to its last aircraft or pilot. At the finish there remained about 3,500 aircraft, but most of these sat at their dispersals with their fuel tanks empty. Between 1st September 1939 and 28th February 1945, the last date for which reliable figures exist, the force had lost 44,065 aircrew killed or missing, 28,200 wounded and 27,010 prisoners or missing.

And what if the Luftwaffe had been able to overcome the greatest of the problems which beset it during the war? What if it had been able to attack the mass of Russian industry behind the Ural Mountains with its own long-range heavy bombers? What if Hitler had allowed the Me 262 to go into large scale service as a fighter in the late spring of 1944? What if the Luftwaffe training organisation had not broken down? What if its fuel supplies had remained intact, and sufficient synthetic refining capacity had been available to meet all needs? What then? Then the war might have continued on for a little longer, but the outcome would have been the same. For had the Germans fought on until August 1945 it is likely that the horror of the atomic bomb would have forced them to surrender, just as it forced the capitulation of the even more obdurate Japanese.

157

Appendix 1

FORMATION OR OFFICE	RANK OF COMMANDER
Oberbefehlshaber der Luftwaffe (Supreme Commander)	Reichmarschall
Chef des Generalstabes der Luftwaffe (Chief of Air Staff)	General der Flieger or Generaloberst
Luftflotte (Air Force)	General der Flieger or Generalfeldmarschall
Fliegerkorps (Air Corps)	General der Flieger or Generalleutnant
Fliegerdivision (Air Division)	General der Flieger, Generalleutnant or Generalmajor
Geschwader (Group)	Generalmajor, Oberst, Oberstleutnant or Major, with courtesy title of Kommodore
Gruppe (Wing)	Oberstleutnant, Major or Hauptmann with courtesy title of Kommandeur
Staffel (Squadron)	Hauptmann or Oberleutnant with courtesy title of Kapitän

When using this tabulation, it must be remembered that the pattern could be altered according to the size and nature of the campaign being fought, and consequently this is only an approximate chain of command.

Appendix 2

EQUIVALENT COMMISSIONED RANKS

Luftwaffe	Royal Air Force	United States Air Force
Generalfeldmarschall	Marshal of the Royal Air Force	General of the Air Force
Generaloberst	Air Chief Marshal	General
General	Air Marshal	Lieutenant-General
Generalleutnant	Air Vice-Marshal	Major-General
Generalmajor	Air Commodore	Brigadier-General
Oberst	Group Captain	Colonel
Oberstleutnant	Wing Commander	Lieutenant-Colonel
Major	Squadron Leader	Major
Hauptmann	Flight Lieutenant	Captain
Oberleutnant	Flying Officer	Lieutenant
Leutnant	Pilot Officer	Second-Lieutenant

Appendix 3

THE ORGANISATION AND NOMENCLATURE OF LUFTWAFFE UNITS

The basic unit of the Luftwaffe was not the *Staffel* or squadron, but the *Gruppe* or wing, which could, and often did, act independently of the *Geschwader* or group to which it nominally belonged. Despite this, however, nomenclature of Luftwaffe units was derived from the *Geschwader*, and thus we should start with this unit in an analysis of the composition of Luftwaffe tactical units.

Each *Geschwader* was normally composed of three *Gruppen*, although some fighter *Geschwader* had four *Gruppen* and some bomber ones up to six *Gruppen*. Each *Gruppe* was made up of three *Staffeln* in the normal course of events. Each *Staffel* was usually composed of between twelve and sixteen aircraft, so that the strength of the *Gruppe* was about forty and the *Geschwader* about 120 aircraft. Of course front line combat units were frequently far below establishment strengths, so these figures must always be regarded warily.

The abbreviated nomenclature of Luftwaffe units is sufficiently clear for the exact unit to be deciphered from the short abridgement of its full title. In the middle of the abbreviation was an oblique stroke, to the right of which appeared letters signifying the role of the unit (for the meaning of these letters see below). To the right again of these was the *Geschwader's* official number and sometimes an honour title such as 'Udet' or 'Eismeer'. To the left of the oblique stroke appeared either Roman or Arabic numerals, the Roman numerals referring to the *Gruppe*, the Arabic to the *Staffel*. As the *Staffeln* were arranged into *Gruppen* by threes, it can be seen that *Staffeln 1* to *3* belonged to *I Gruppe*, *4* to *6* to *II Gruppe* and so on. Thus when presented with a designation such as *9/JG 54 Grünherz*, we can see that this refers to the third *Staffel* of the *Gruppe* of *Jagdgeschwader 54*, honour title Grünherz.

Aufkl Gr = Aufklärungsgruppe = Reconnaissance wing
E Gr = Erprobungsgruppe = Testing wing
JG = Jagdgeschwader = Fighter group
K Fl Gr = Küstenfliegergruppe = Coastal wing
KG = Kampfgeschwader = Bomber group
KLG = Kampflehrgeschwader = Bomber training group
LG = Lehrgeschwader = (literally) Training group, in fact an elite unit
NJG = Nachtjagdgeschwader = Night fighter group
NSG = Nachtschlachtgeschwader = Night ground support group
SG = Schlachtgeschwader = Ground support group
SKG = Schnellkampfgeschwader = Fast bomber group
St G = Stukageschwader = Dive bomber group
TG = Transportgeschwader = Transport group
ZG = Zerstörergeschwader = Long range or escort fighter group
zbV = zur besonderen Verwendung = Special assignment.

It must always be borne in mind that the translation of the Luftwaffe units German names is only an approximate one.

Bibliography

The Author wishes to thank Messrs Ian Allan Ltd for permission to use material originally researched for his book 'Pictorial History of the Luftwaffe'; Evans Bros Ltd for permission to quote the passage from the book 'I Flew For The Führer'; Fontana Books for permission to quote from 'The Struggle For Europe'; and Her Majesty's Stationery Officer for permission to use material from the unpublished history 'The Rise And Fa Of The German Air Force'.

Instruments of Darkness Alfred Price (William Kimber, London)
Pictorial History of the Luftwaffe Alfred Price (Ian Allan)
German Air Force Bombers of World War Two (Two Volumes) Alfred Price (Hylton Lacy)
The Struggle for Europe Chester Wilmot (Collins, London, Harper & Row, New York)
The First And The Last Adolf Galland (Methuen, London. Holt, New York)
USAF Staff Histories, Arno Press Inc: *Historical Turning Points in the German Air Force War Effort, The German Air Force Versus Russia, 1941, 1942, 1943 (3 Volumes), The German Air Force General Staff, German Air Operations In Support Of The Army*
The Mare's Nest David Irving (William Kimber, London. Little Brown, Bosto
Duel Under The Stars Wilhelm Johnen (William Kimber, London. Ace Books, New York, as Battle of the Bombers)
Broken Swastika Werner Baumbach (Robert Hale, London. Coward McCann, New York)
I Flew For The Führer Heinz Knoke (Evans Bros, London, Rinehart & Winston, New York)